P.57 — salad

The EatingWell RUSH HOUR COOKBOOK

A Very Valencian Menu
Page 158

The EatingWell RUSH HOUR COOKBOOK

Healthy Meals for Busy Cooks

By the Editors of

EatingWell

The Magazine of Food & Health

EatingWell
BOOKS

A division of Eating Well Magazine
Box 1001, Ferry Road, Charlotte, Vermont 05445-1001

EATING WELL: The Magazine of Food & Health®
is a registered trademark of EATING WELL® Magazine.
For subscription information, write to EATING WELL, P.O. Box 54263, Boulder, CO 80322-4263
or call 1-800-EAT-WELL.

Library of Congress Cataloging-in-Publication Data

The Eating well rush hour cookbook: healthy meals for busy cooks / from the editors of Eating well.

p.   cm.
Includes index.
ISBN 1-884943-05-5 (hardcover) — ISBN 1-884943-06-3 (softcover)
1. Quick and easy cookery.   2. Low-fat diet—Recipes.   3. Menus.
I. Eating well.
TX833.5.E28   1994   94-20771
641.5'55—dc20   CIP

Editorial Director: Scott Mowbray
Coordinating Editor: Cheryl Dorschner   **Production Editor:** Wendy S. Ruopp
Recipe Editor: Susan Herr   **Test Kitchen Director:** Patsy Jamieson
Food Editor: Susan Stuck   **Nutrition Editor:** Elizabeth Hiser
Special Contributors: Amy Bennett (*Writer*), Karen Brasel (*Nutritionist*), Sharon L. Smith (*Indexer*), David Grist (*Permissions*)

Art Director: Joannah Ralston   **Designer:** Gregg Stacy
Photography Stylist: Betty Alfenito   **Food Stylist:** Anne Disrude
Photographer: Steven Mark Needham   **Illustrator:** Timothy Carroll
Front cover photograph: "Great Garlicky Chicken" menu (page 151)

Distributed by
Artisan, a Division of Workman Publishing
708 Broadway
New York, NY 10003

Printed and bound in Canada by
Friesen & Sons
Altona, Manitoba

Acknowledgments

We would like to express our gratitude to a diverse and dedicated group of cooks and food-lovers for their work on this project.

Susanne Davis and Alison Frye in the EATING WELL test kitchen for their repeated and tireless efforts at making the recipes work flawlessly.

Recipe developers Lisa Cherkasky and Marie Piraino, whose creative minds, quick hands and slightly raucous humor lightened the load.

The enthusiastic group of EATING WELL subscribers who tested menus, invited friends over to taste, and gave us lots of valuable feedback:

Lara Broom, Janie Cohen, Jennifer Francois, Sally Gottfried, Joan Hanley, Marc Maderazzo, Maryanne Michaels, Karen Molinaroli, Radetta Nemcosky.

Suzanne Seibel, who spotted our mistakes and inconsistencies.

Asa Aaron Mease, who waited to be born until his mother, Cheryl Dorschner, had completed work on the manuscript.

Contents

Autumn

Winter

Introduction

Be Quick, Be Healthy

We are often exasperated by the thousand and one demands of modern life—usually just about the time we have to cook dinner. On weeknights especially, spending less time in the kitchen becomes a clear necessity if we are to spend more time at the table, enjoying food and family. Too often, in the rush, something is compromised: taste, health or the whole joy of making and eating a home-cooked meal.

EATING WELL Magazine is dedicated to serving up food that tastes good and is healthy too. Our *Rush Hour* menu column has long been a favorite of readers. Here we emphasize not only taste and health (the nutritional facts are always listed), but time (a meal prepared in an hour or less). For we know this about our readers: just because they need to cook quickly doesn't mean they don't love to cook. And there is a special satisfaction in getting a good meal to the table in short order.

Today's supermarkets carry an unprecedented range of foods, and that has really opened the door to much more interesting quick cooking. We take full advantage of this rich variety, visiting the produce section for shiitake mushrooms or jícama, the specialty food shelves for sauces, noodles, spices. That said, we have aimed for ease and speed, and have given alternative ingredients wherever possible.

The menus in this book take their inspiration from a wealth of cuisines. Mediterranean food—Italian in particular—with its emphasis on vegetables, grains, pasta and small portions of meat, is a natural source for the EATING WELL style of cooking. Asian influences can be found throughout, and Asian condiments are often used to heighten flavors in these low-fat recipes. American standards are not forgotten; burgers, barbecue and chili all find their way into healthful *Rush Hour* menus.

You will not find fancy or fussy desserts in this book. Most meals end with jazzed-up fruit. Nutritionally, this is sound—and who wants a rich, elaborate dessert on a weeknight, anyway? Quick tricks with fresh or dried fruits, frozen yogurt, a pinch of spice or a splash of liqueur and a blender yield a fresh, satisfying punctuation to a healthful meal.

What the Nutritional Numbers Mean

Our menus are built around fundamental, widely recognized healthy-eating guidelines: no more than 30 percent of calories in the overall diet should come from fat, and meals should contain modest meat portions in combination with plenty of fruits, vegetables and grains. All the menus in this book derive 30 percent or less of their calories from fat; two-fifths of them derive less than 20 percent of calories from fat.

Total calories, along with calories from fat in the complete menu, are listed on the opening page of each menu. In addition, each recipe features its own nutritional analysis of calories, protein, fat, carbohydrate, sodium and cholesterol for one serving—useful if you're planning to mix and match recipes from different menus to create a menu of your own.

How the Menus & Recipes Work

In each menu, the separate recipes have been designed to form a pleasing whole of contrasting tastes, textures and colors. Each menu consists of three, and occasionally four, simple recipes; suggested additional accompaniments are listed in parentheses. The timetable given with each menu is a clear guide to the most efficient way to produce the meal, so you don't waste valuable time waiting for one element to cook before beginning another.

A note about using the microwave: Power levels are given in recipes in words and percentages (except for high, which is always 100 percent). Because power-level terminology varies from oven to oven, check the owner's manual and use whichever word or number results in the same *percentage* as in the recipe. Our recipes have been tested in a 700-watt full-sized microwave oven. If your oven is different, cooking times may have to be adjusted slightly. If your microwave has a turntable, you may not have to rotate dishes during cooking.

How This Book Works

There are 60 menus in this book, 15 for each season. Menus are listed on the table of contents (page 6) and in more detail on the menu lists for each chapter (pages 10, 62, 116 and 168). The menus are organized to take advantage of fresh seasonal fruits, vegetables, fish and seafood, but the availability of many foods year-round allows you to make your menu choices from any section.

There is a short section at the back of this cookbook called "The Well-Stocked Kitchen." It describes ingredients that may be unfamiliar to some readers, and gives suggestions for where those items can be found.

Spring Menus

Risotto Primavera - 13

Risotto with Spring Vegetables • Salad of Bitter Greens & Walnuts • Coffee-Cognac Coupe

A Taste of the Keys - 16

Pork Tenderloin with Keys Mango Sauce • Braised Scallions & Peas • (Rice)
Banana Split with Caramel Sauce

Light Twist on a Classic - 19

Chicken Cordon Bleu • Zucchini Rice • Sautéed Cherry Tomatoes with Chives
(Sliced Melon)

Quick Salmon Sauté - 22

Salmon with Cucumbers & Dill • Crushed Red Potatoes with Buttermilk
Pineapple with Mango Coulis

Uptown Tuesday Night - 26

Peppered Lamb Chops • Rhubarb Chutney • New Potatoes & Sugar Snap Peas
(Raspberry Sorbet with Sliced Kiwi)

Moroccan Grill - 28

Moroccan Chicken Kebabs • Whole-Wheat Couscous Pilaf • Orange & Black Olive Salad

¡Enchiladas! - 32

Turkey & Bean Enchiladas • Jícama Slaw • Strawberry-Margarita Ice

Lighthearted Chicken - 35

Apple-Ginger Chicken • Lemon Rice • Sesame Green Beans • (Sliced Papaya)

A Pan-Roast with Pasta - 39

Fusilli with Roasted Shrimp, Tomatoes & Asparagus • Tossed Salad with Parmesan Vinaigrette
(French Bread) • Fresh Berry Gratin

Quick Passage to India - 42

Pepper & Egg Curry • (Basmati Rice) • Pineapple-Mint Salad • Pistachio-Cardamom Thins

Fast Soup from the Far East - 45

Chinese Seafood Soup • Spicy Broccoli Salad • Fruit Compote with Coconut
(Fortune Cookies)

Pasta & Tomato Sauce I - 49

Fettuccine with Fresh Tuna Sauce • Roasted Asparagus • Stewed Rhubarb with Orange

Dinner at the Oasis - 52

Vegetable Tagine with Couscous • Romaine & Fresh Herb Salad
Apricot Whip with Raspberries

Spring Frittata - 55

Asparagus Frittata • Chickpea & Red Onion Salad • (Italian Bread) • Strawberry Shortcakes

Bowlful of Fragrant Mussels - 59

Steamed Mussels in Tomato Broth • (French Bread) • Herb Sauce • Maple Custards

Risotto Primavera

lump Italian arborio rice gives risotto its distinctive taste and creamy texture. In this entrée, it is combined with an assortment of vegetables and enriched with Parmesan cheese to make a colorful spring dish. The recipe is easily made vegetarian by substituting vegetable for chicken broth. Challenging the mild risotto is a salad made with pleasingly bitter greens. The low-fat dressing combines tarragon vinegar, finely chopped shallots and a little walnut oil. The oil's unique flavor is brought forward by the toasted walnuts sprinkled over the top of the salad. The Coffee-Cognac Coupe is an elegant finale; the darkly intense sauce contrasts wonderfully with the frozen yogurt.

MENU

·····························

Risotto with
Spring Vegetables

Salad of
Bitter Greens
& Walnuts

Coffee-Cognac
Coupe

Risotto with Spring Vegetables

5½-6½	cups defatted reduced-sodium chicken stock
16	baby carrots (6 oz.), trimmed, peeled and cut in half lengthwise
16	thin stalks or 8 medium-sized stalks asparagus (6 oz.), trimmed and cut into 2-inch lengths
1	cup sugar snap peas (4 oz.), trimmed, strings removed
1	9-oz. pkg. frozen artichoke hearts
2	tsp. olive oil
1	onion, chopped
1	clove garlic, finely chopped
1½	cups arborio rice (*see* "The Well-Stocked Kitchen" *on page 221*)
½	cup dry white wine
1½	Tbsp. chopped fresh thyme or 1½ tsp. dried thyme leaves
¾	cup freshly grated Parmesan cheese
	salt & freshly ground black pepper to taste

THIS MENU CONTAINS
809 CALORIES
PER SERVING WITH
17% OF CALORIES
FROM FAT.

Timetable

....

1. *Make coffee sauce for dessert.*

2. *Wash salad greens.*

3. *Toast walnuts for salad.*

4. *Mix salad dressing.*

5. *Make risotto.*

In a medium-sized saucepan, bring stock to a boil over medium heat. Add carrots and cook 3 to 5 minutes, until almost tender. Add asparagus and peas and cook for 1 minute longer. With a slotted spoon, remove the vegetables to a bowl to cool. Reduce heat to maintain the stock at a gentle simmer. Place artichoke hearts in a sieve and thaw under warm water; set aside.

In a Dutch oven or large, wide saucepan, heat oil over medium-low heat. Add onions and garlic and cook, stirring, until softened, 3 to 5 minutes. Add rice and stir to coat grains. Add wine and cook, stirring frequently, until most of the liquid has been absorbed, 2 to 3 minutes. Add ½ cup of the simmering stock and cook, stirring frequently, until most of the liquid has been absorbed, 2 to 3 minutes more. Continue adding stock ½ cup at a time, stirring frequently, until the rice begins to soften, about 15 minutes. Stir in the reserved artichoke hearts and thyme, adding more stock as needed, until the mixture is creamy, about 5 minutes more. Stir in the reserved vegetables and cheese. Season with salt and pepper.

Serves 4.

518 CALORIES PER SERVING: 20 G PROTEIN, 9 G FAT, 86 G CARBOHYDRATE; 459 MG SODIUM; 16 MG CHOLESTEROL.

Salad of Bitter Greens & Walnuts

2 Tbsp. chopped walnuts
2 Tbsp. defatted reduced-sodium chicken stock
1 Tbsp. tarragon vinegar or white-wine vinegar
1 Tbsp. walnut oil or olive oil, preferably extra-virgin
1 Tbsp. finely chopped shallots
1 tsp. Dijon mustard
   salt & freshly ground black pepper to taste
8 cups washed, dried and torn mixed greens, such as escarole, chicory and/or radicchio

In a small dry skillet over low heat, stir walnuts until lightly toasted, about 3 minutes. Transfer to a plate to cool.

In a large salad bowl, whisk together chicken stock, vinegar, oil, shallots, mustard, salt and pepper. Add greens and toss thoroughly. Sprinkle with the walnuts and additional black pepper to taste.

Serves 4.

76 CALORIES PER SERVING: 2 G PROTEIN, 6 G FAT, 5 G CARBOHYDRATE; 11 MG SODIUM; 0 MG CHOLESTEROL.

Coffee-Cognac Coupe

⅓ cup sugar

2 tsp. instant coffee powder

2 Tbsp. cognac or brandy

3 cups nonfat vanilla frozen yogurt

In a small saucepan, combine sugar, coffee powder and ¼ cup water. Bring to a boil over medium heat, stirring to dissolve the sugar. Boil until slightly thickened, 2 to 3 minutes. Remove from heat and stir in cognac. Let cool.

Just before serving, in 4 parfait or dessert glasses, alternate layers of sauce and frozen yogurt, beginning and ending with sauce.

Serves 4.

215 CALORIES PER SERVING: 6 G PROTEIN, 0 G FAT, 44 G CARBOHYDRATE; 119 MG SODIUM; 0 MG CHOLESTEROL.

A Taste of the Keys

MENU

....

*Pork Tenderloin
with Keys
Mango Sauce*

*Braised Scallions
& Peas*

(Rice)

*Banana Split with
Caramel Sauce*

THIS MENU CONTAINS
773 CALORIES
PER SERVING WITH
12% OF CALORIES
FROM FAT.

Mangoes have the power to transform a familiar dish into something extraordinary. Lustrous in shades of gold, crimson and dusky purple, their flesh is scented with notes of peach and pine, citrus and honey. More than just a pretty fruit, mangoes are high in vitamin C as well. Here, in a recipe from Florida cooking expert Linda Gassenheimer, mango flesh is pureed with ginger and sherry, and spooned onto a platter; thin pork tenderloin slices are arranged on top. The scallions are a pleasant surprise braised with peas for the side dish. And for dessert, cooking the bananas brings out their inherent sweetness; topped with nonfat frozen yogurt and caramel sauce, they close the meal deliciously.

Pork Tenderloin with Keys Mango Sauce

2½ cups diced fresh mango (2 mangoes)
 ⅓ cup sugar
 3 Tbsp. red-wine vinegar
 3 Tbsp. dry sherry
1½ Tbsp. finely chopped fresh ginger
     salt & freshly ground black pepper to taste
 1 lb. pork tenderloin, trimmed of fat and membrane
 1 tsp. vegetable oil, preferably canola oil
 1 tsp. chopped fresh rosemary or ½ tsp. crushed dried, plus fresh sprigs for garnish (optional)
 1 tsp. chopped fresh thyme or ½ tsp. dried thyme leaves, plus fresh sprigs for garnish (optional)

Preheat oven to 400 degrees F. In a food processor or blender, puree mangoes. (If the mangoes are stringy, strain the puree through a fine sieve.) Transfer to a medium-sized heavy saucepan and stir in sugar, vinegar, sherry and ginger. Heat over low heat, stirring to dissolve sugar; do not boil the puree. Remove from heat and season with salt and pepper.

Brush pork with oil and sprinkle with rosemary, thyme, salt and pepper. Place pork on a lightly oiled rack in a roasting pan and roast for 10 minutes. Reduce oven heat to 325 degrees F and roast for 10 to 15 minutes more, or until the internal temperature registers 160 degrees F and the pork is no longer pink inside. Transfer to a carving board, cover with aluminum foil and let stand for 10 minutes.

Carve the pork into ¼-inch-thick slices. Spoon a little mango sauce onto a platter or 4 plates and lay pork slices on top. Serve the remaining sauce alongside. Garnish with rosemary and/or thyme sprigs if desired.

Serves 4.

297 CALORIES PER SERVING: 25 G PROTEIN, 6 G FAT, 36 G CARBOHYDRATE; 60 MG SODIUM; 79 MG CHOLESTEROL.

Braised Scallions & Peas

2 tsp. olive oil

2 bunches scallions, washed, trimmed and cut crosswise into thirds

1 cup fresh or frozen peas

salt & freshly ground black pepper to taste

In a medium-sized skillet, heat oil over medium heat. Add scallions with water still clinging to them and cover. Reduce heat to low and cook until scallions are almost tender, about 3 minutes. Stir in peas, cover and cook until peas are heated through, about 2 more minutes. Season with salt and pepper.

Serves 4.

55 CALORIES PER SERVING: 2 G PROTEIN, 2 G FAT, 7 G CARBOHYDRATE; 35 MG SODIUM; 0 MG CHOLESTEROL.

Timetable

1. Preheat oven to 400 degrees F.

2. Make mango sauce.

3. Roast pork.

4. Make caramel sauce for dessert.

5. Cook rice.

6. Cook scallions and peas.

7. Preheat broiler for dessert.

Banana Split with Caramel Sauce

½ cup sugar

1½ tsp. butter

⅓ cup evaporated skim milk

¼ tsp. pure vanilla extract

4 large firm bananas

1 pt. nonfat vanilla frozen yogurt

In a small heavy saucepan, bring sugar and ¼ cup water to a boil, stirring occasionally. Cook over medium-high heat, without stirring, until the syrup turns amber, 5 to 10 minutes. (Take care not to burn it.)

Remove from the heat and cool for 2 minutes. Using a wooden spoon, stir in butter. Gradually stir in evaporated milk. Return to the heat and cook, stirring, until the caramel is dissolved, about 1 minute. Stir in vanilla and set aside to cool.

Preheat broiler. Lightly oil a baking sheet or coat with nonstick cooking spray. Peel bananas and cut in half lengthwise. Place on a baking sheet, cut-side up, and brush with some of the caramel sauce. Broil until lightly colored, 3 to 4 minutes. Place bananas in serving dishes, add a scoop of frozen yogurt and top with the caramel sauce.

Serves 4.

318 CALORIES PER SERVING: 5 G PROTEIN, 2 G FAT, 75 G CARBOHYDRATE; 107 MG SODIUM; 5 MG CHOLESTEROL.

Light Twist on a Classic

Veal Cordon Bleu is standard on menus in Switzerland, but this *Rush Hour* chicken version is much lower in fat. Dipped twice for extra crunch, it's golden and crisp without, melted and tender within. The Gruyère and prosciutto are both intensely flavorful; a little of each goes a long way. Simple but unusual, the rice side dish is spangled with zucchini and subtly scented with lemon zest. The cherry tomatoes are cooked just enough to be heated through, then tossed with fresh chives. Both side dishes are beautiful on the plate next to the chicken. Slice a fragrant cantaloupe or Persian melon for dessert.

Chicken Cordon Bleu

1 lb. boneless, skinless chicken breasts, fat trimmed (4 breast halves)

2 oz. prosciutto (*see* "The Well-Stocked Kitchen" *on page 221*), thinly sliced and cut into ½-inch strips

2 oz. Gruyère cheese, thinly sliced and cut into ½-inch strips

2 large egg whites

¼ cup buttermilk

1 Tbsp. Dijon mustard

⅔ cup fine, dry unseasoned breadcrumbs

¼ cup freshly grated Parmesan cheese

½ tsp. salt

½ tsp. freshly ground black pepper

4 lemon wedges

Preheat oven to 400 degrees F. Lightly oil a rack large enough to hold chicken breasts in a single layer. Put the rack on a baking sheet and set aside.

MENU

Chicken Cordon Bleu

Zucchini Rice

Sautéed Cherry Tomatoes with Chives

(Sliced Melon)

THIS MENU CONTAINS 613 CALORIES PER SERVING WITH 25% OF CALORIES FROM FAT.

Timetable

....

1. *Preheat oven to 400 degrees F.*

2. *Prepare and bake chicken breasts.*

3. *Make rice.*

4. *Sauté cherry tomatoes.*

To prepare the chicken breasts for stuffing, place a breast half, skinned-side down, on a cutting board. Keeping the blade of a sharp knife parallel to the work surface, make a horizontal slit along the thinner, long edge of each breast, cutting nearly through to the opposite side.

Open the breast so it forms two flaps, hinged at the center. Place one-quarter of the prosciutto and Gruyère on one half breast, leaving a ½-inch space between the filling and the edges of the breast. Close the chicken carefully and set aside. Repeat with the remaining chicken breasts.

In a medium-sized bowl, combine egg whites, buttermilk and mustard and beat with a whisk until creamy. In a shallow dish, stir together breadcrumbs, Parmesan, salt and pepper.

Carefully dip each piece of chicken in the crumb mixture, then in the egg-white mixture, and back again in the crumb mixture. Set on the prepared rack and bake for 30 to 35 minutes, until crisp and lightly browned on the outside and opaque in the center. Serve with lemon wedges.

Serves 4.

325 CALORIES PER SERVING: 40 G PROTEIN, 11 G FAT, 14 G CARBOHYDRATE; 814 MG SODIUM; 97 MG CHOLESTEROL.

Zucchini Rice

....

2 tsp. olive oil
⅓ cup chopped shallots (about 2 large shallots)
1½ cups defatted reduced-sodium chicken stock
1 cup long-grain white rice
2 cups finely diced zucchini (1 medium)
2 tsp. grated lemon zest
½ tsp. salt
¼ tsp. freshly ground black pepper

Conventional Method: In a medium-sized saucepan, heat oil over medium heat. Add shallots and cook, stirring, until softened, about 2 minutes. Add chicken stock and bring to a simmer. Stir in rice, zucchini, lemon zest, salt and pepper. Reduce heat to low, cover pan and cook until the rice is tender and all the liquid is absorbed, 15 to 17 minutes. Fluff with a fork before serving.

Microwave Method: In a microwave-safe 2½-qt. casserole, combine oil and shallots; microwave on high power for 2 to 3 minutes, until softened. Add chicken stock, rice, lemon zest, salt and pepper. Cover casserole with a lid or vented plastic wrap and microwave on high power for 5 minutes. Stir once, cover and microwave on medium power (50 percent), without stirring, for 7 minutes; add zucchini and cook an additional 3 to 5 minutes, or until the rice is tender. Let stand, covered, for 5 minutes. Fluff with a fork before serving.

Serves 4.

208 CALORIES PER SERVING: 4 G PROTEIN, 3 G FAT, 41 G CARBOHYDRATE; 273 MG SODIUM; 0 MG CHOLESTEROL.

Sautéed Cherry Tomatoes with Chives

2   tsp. olive oil
2   pts. cherry tomatoes
2   Tbsp. chopped fresh chives
    salt & freshly ground black pepper to taste

In a large skillet, heat oil over medium-high heat. Add tomatoes and sauté until skins begin to split, 3 to 4 minutes. Remove from heat, toss with chives and season with salt and pepper.

Serves 4.

52 CALORIES PER SERVING: 1 G PROTEIN, 3 G FAT, 7 G CARBOHYDRATE; 12 MG SODIUM; 0 MG CHOLESTEROL.

Quick Salmon Sauté

MENU
....

*Salmon with
Cucumbers
& Dill*

*Crushed
Red Potatoes
with Buttermilk*

*Pineapple with
Mango Coulis*

THIS MENU CONTAINS
403 CALORIES
PER SERVING WITH
22% OF CALORIES
FROM FAT.

The trinity of salmon, cucumbers and dill takes on a new form for tonight's main course. Seared first to lock in moisture, the fish is then combined with braised cucumbers—an unexpected yet delicious way to enjoy that vegetable's subtle flavor. The potatoes are even easier than mashed—simply crushed, then enlivened with tart buttermilk and fresh spring chives. A golden mango sauce, deepened with dark rum, lends a lovely tropical accent to pineapple for dessert.

Salmon with Cucumbers & Dill

2	seedless (European) cucumbers (1½ lbs.), washed and trimmed
2	Tbsp. all-purpose white flour
¼	tsp. salt, plus more to taste
¼	tsp. freshly ground black pepper, plus more to taste
1½	lbs. skinless salmon fillets, preferably center-cut, cut into 1½-inch cubes
4	tsp. olive oil
⅓	cup defatted reduced-sodium chicken stock
	pinch sugar
¼	cup chopped fresh dill, plus sprigs for garnish
	lemon wedges for garnish

Cut cucumbers into 2-inch-by-½-inch sticks and set aside.

In a shallow dish, combine flour, salt and pepper. Dredge salmon pieces in the flour mixture, shaking off the excess.

In a large nonstick skillet, heat 2 tsp. of the oil over high heat. Add half of the salmon pieces and sauté them until lightly browned on the outside but still pink inside, 4 to 5 minutes. Transfer the salmon to a

Timetable

....

1. *Cut pineapple;*
   make mango sauce.

2. *Boil potatoes.*

3. *Prepare and cook*
   salmon.

4. *Finish potatoes.*

plate and set aside.

Wipe out the skillet with paper towels, add the remaining 2 tsp. oil and return the pan to the heat. Add the remaining salmon and sauté in the same manner. Set aside.

Wipe out the skillet again and add the reserved cucumbers, stock and sugar. Season with salt and pepper and bring to a simmer over medium heat. Cover and simmer until the cucumbers are tender-crisp, 3 to 4 minutes.

Remove the cover, increase heat to high and boil until the pan juices are reduced to 2 Tbsp., about 3 minutes. Add the reserved salmon and dill to the skillet and simmer, covered, just until the salmon is opaque in the center, 2 to 3 minutes.

Taste and adjust seasonings. Garnish with dill sprigs and lemon wedges.

Serves 6.

216 CALORIES PER SERVING: 24 G PROTEIN, 10 G FAT, 6 G CARBOHYDRATE; 164 MG SODIUM; 63 MG CHOLESTEROL.

Crushed Red Potatoes with Buttermilk

....

- 2 lbs. red potatoes, scrubbed (about 6 potatoes)
- 1 tsp. salt, plus more to taste
- ½ cup buttermilk
- 2 Tbsp. chopped fresh chives
     freshly ground black pepper to taste

In a large saucepan, cover potatoes with cold water. Add salt and bring to a simmer over medium heat. Cook until tender, 12 to 15 minutes. Drain the potatoes in a colander and transfer to a medium-sized bowl. Coarsely crush the potatoes with a potato masher or the back of a large spoon. Gently stir in buttermilk and chives. Season with salt and pepper.

Serves 6.

126 CALORIES PER SERVING: 3 G PROTEIN, 0 G FAT, 28 G CARBOHYDRATE; 382 MG SODIUM; 1 MG CHOLESTEROL.

Pineapple with Mango Coulis

Fresh mango is best here, but if you cannot find a ripe one, use jarred mango.

 1 ripe pineapple, skinned and cored
¾ cup diced fresh mango (1 small mango)
1½ Tbsp. dark rum
1½ Tbsp. lime juice
 1 tsp. grated lime zest
 1 Tbsp. sugar, or to taste
    fresh mint sprigs for garnish

Cut pineapple into spears or chunks and set aside.

In a food processor or blender, puree mango pieces, rum, lime juice and zest. Add sugar to taste.

Arrange the pineapple in serving bowls and top with the sauce. Garnish with mint sprigs.

Serves 6.

61 CALORIES PER SERVING: 0 G PROTEIN, 0 G FAT, 14 G CARBOHYDRATE; 2 MG SODIUM; 0 MG CHOLESTEROL.

Uptown Tuesday Night

MENU

....

*Peppered
Lamb Chops*

Rhubarb Chutney

*New Potatoes &
Sugar Snap Peas*

*(Raspberry Sorbet
with Sliced Kiwi)*

THIS MENU CONTAINS
517 CALORIES
PER SERVING WITH
26% OF CALORIES
FROM FAT.

The rhubarb is up in the garden and your tax refund has arrived. Why not celebrate with broiled spring lamb chops, served not with a staid mint jelly but with a sprightly Rhubarb Chutney? Before cooking, the chops are coated with cracked peppercorns, which produces a crunchy outer coating and meltingly tender meat. New potatoes and sugar snap peas continue the fresh spirit of the meal. If you like, serve a scoop of raspberry sorbet with some kiwi slices on the top for dessert—the color contrast is quite pretty.

Peppered Lamb Chops

....

12   4-oz. loin or rib lamb chops, fat trimmed, approximately 1-inch thick

2   cloves garlic, slivered

1   tsp. olive oil

1   tsp. black peppercorns, crushed with a heavy pot

Preheat the broiler. Pat lamb chops dry. Insert slivers of garlic into each one, making small punctures with a paring knife and poking in the garlic. Brush the tops lightly with half of the olive oil, then pat on half of the cracked peppercorns. Repeat with the other side of the lamb, using remaining oil and peppercorns. Broil the chops for 3 to 4 minutes per side, until the lamb is browned but pink inside.

Serves 6.

208 CALORIES PER SERVING: 24 G PROTEIN, 12 G FAT, 1 G CARBOHYDRATE; 73 MG SODIUM; 77 MG CHOLESTEROL.

Rhubarb Chutney

½ lb. rhubarb, trimmed and cut into ½-inch pieces (2 cups)
½ onion, chopped
⅓ cup honey
¼ cup golden raisins
2 jalapeño peppers, seeded and finely chopped
1 Tbsp. cider vinegar
1 clove garlic, finely chopped
   pinch of ground cardamom or ginger

Mix all ingredients in a medium-sized saucepan with ¼ cup water. Bring to a simmer over medium heat; reduce heat to low, cover pan and cook for 15 minutes. Uncover and cook until thick, 3 to 5 more minutes.
   Serves 6.

91 CALORIES PER SERVING: 1 G PROTEIN, 0 G FAT, 23 G CARBOHYDRATE; 4 MG SODIUM; 0 MG CHOLESTEROL.

New Potatoes & Sugar Snap Peas

1 lb. new potatoes, unpeeled, scrubbed
1 tsp. salt, plus more to taste
2 cups sugar snap peas, strings removed
2 tsp. butter
½ tsp. freshly ground black pepper, plus more to taste
2 Tbsp. chopped fresh mint

Place potatoes in a small saucepan, cover with water and add salt; bring to a boil. Cook over medium heat just until tender, 5 to 6 minutes. Add peas, cover and cook for 2 minutes more. Drain, add butter, pepper and mint. Heat for 1 minute and toss gently. Season with salt and pepper.
   Serves 6.

98 CALORIES PER SERVING: 3 G PROTEIN, 2 G FAT, 19 G CARBOHYDRATE; 402 MG SODIUM; 4 MG CHOLESTEROL.

Timetable

1. Make chutney.

2. Preheat broiler.

3. Season lamb chops.

4. Prepare sugar snaps.

5. Cook potatoes.

6. Broil chops.

Moroccan Grill

MENU

....

*Moroccan
Chicken Kebabs*

*Whole-Wheat
Couscous Pilaf*

*Orange & Black
Olive Salad*

THIS MENU CONTAINS
508 CALORIES
PER SERVING WITH
16% OF CALORIES
FROM FAT.

These North African-inspired chicken kebabs are marinated just 20 minutes in nonfat yogurt blended with a vibrant combination of fresh cilantro, lemon juice, garlic and spices; the chicken is then threaded on skewers with zucchini and red and yellow peppers and grilled. The vegetables are blanched first, so they will be tender after only a short time over the flame. Serve the bright, flavorful kebabs on a bed of slightly spicy couscous. It's worth looking for whole-wheat couscous, which has a distinctly nutty flavor. The salad, one of many versions of a Moroccan classic, is a simple but dramatic combination of peeled orange segments accented with chopped black olives and mint. It is a cool contrast to the spice and the heat of the entrée.

Moroccan Chicken Kebabs

¼ cup nonfat plain yogurt

¼ cup chopped fresh parsley

2 Tbsp. chopped fresh cilantro

2 Tbsp. lemon juice

1 Tbsp. olive oil

3 cloves garlic, finely chopped

1½ tsp. paprika

1 tsp. ground cumin

¼ tsp. salt

¼ tsp. freshly ground black pepper

1 lb. boneless, skinless chicken breasts, fat trimmed, cut into 1-inch pieces

2 small bell peppers (red and/or yellow), cored, seeded and

cut into 1½-inch pieces

1 zucchini, cut into ¼-inch-thick rounds

In a medium-sized bowl, stir together yogurt, parsley, cilantro, lemon juice, olive oil, garlic, paprika, cumin, salt and black pepper. Add chicken and toss to coat well. Cover with plastic wrap and marinate in the refrigerator for 20 minutes. If using wooden skewers for the kebabs, put them in water to soak.

Meanwhile, prepare grill or preheat broiler. Blanch peppers in boiling salted water for 3 minutes. Remove with a slotted spoon and refresh with cold water. Blanch zucchini for 1 minute. Drain and refresh with cold water.

Alternate chicken cubes, peppers and zucchini on skewers. Grill or broil the kebabs until the chicken is no longer pink in the center, 3 to 4 minutes per side.

Serve on a bed of couscous.

Serves 4.

193 CALORIES PER SERVING: 29 G PROTEIN, 5 G FAT, 8 G CARBOHYDRATE; 224 MG SODIUM; 66 MG CHOLESTEROL.

Whole-Wheat Couscous Pilaf

1¼ cups defatted reduced-sodium chicken stock or water

1 Tbsp. butter

½ tsp. Tabasco sauce

¼ tsp. salt, plus more to taste

1½ cups couscous, preferably whole-wheat (*see* "The Well-Stocked Kitchen" *on page 221*)

1 Tbsp. chopped fresh parsley

freshly ground black pepper to taste

In a small saucepan with a tight-fitting lid, combine stock or water, butter, Tabasco sauce and ¼ tsp. salt and bring to a boil. Stir in couscous and remove from heat.

Timetable

1. Marinate chicken.

2. Blanch zucchini, peppers for kebabs.

3. Prepare grill or preheat broiler.

4. Make orange salad.

5. Assemble kebabs.

6. Make couscous.

7. Cook kebabs.

Cover and let stand for 5 minutes. Uncover and fluff the grains with a fork to separate. Stir in parsley. Season with salt and pepper.
 Serves 4.

285 CALORIES PER SERVING: 9 G PROTEIN, 3 G FAT, 53 G CARBOHYDRATE; 172 MG SODIUM; 8 MG CHOLESTEROL.

Orange & Black Olive Salad

 5 Valencia or navel oranges
 ⅓ cup chopped fresh mint
 2 Tbsp. chopped pitted black olives
 1 Tbsp. olive oil, preferably extra-virgin
 1 clove garlic, finely chopped
 ½ tsp. ground coriander
    pinch sugar
    salt to taste
    lettuce leaves

With a sharp knife, remove skin and white pith from oranges and discard. Working over a bowl, cut orange segments from their surrounding membranes and let them fall into the bowl. Squeeze any remaining juice from the membranes into the bowl. Add mint, olives, oil, garlic, coriander and sugar. Season with salt and toss gently. Serve on lettuce leaves.
 Serves 4.

30 CALORIES PER SERVING: 0 G PROTEIN, 1 G FAT, 5 G CARBOHYDRATE; 11 MG SODIUM; 0 MG CHOLESTEROL.

¡Enchiladas!

MENU

Turkey & Bean
Enchiladas

Jícama Slaw

Strawberry-
Margarita Ice

THIS MENU CONTAINS
844 CALORIES
PER SERVING WITH
25% OF CALORIES
FROM FAT.

This enlightened version of enchiladas features a filling of lean ground turkey and pinto beans. Before rolling the enchiladas, corn tortillas are softened, not in hot lard as is traditional, but by passing them briefly over the heat of a stovetop burner. The heat of the flame imparts a rich, toasted flavor to the corn. An off-the-shelf salsa provides heat of a spicy kind to these robust enchiladas. The food processor helps make short work of fixing this meal. First whirl frozen fruit, sugar and a splash of tequila in the processor bowl, then scoop the mixture into margarita glasses and freeze. Rinse the bowl and change the blade to a grating disk to prepare the slaw.

Turkey & Bean Enchiladas

½ lb. ground turkey
2 tsp. vegetable oil, preferably canola oil
1 onion, chopped
3 cloves garlic, finely chopped
1-2 jalapeño peppers, cored, seeded and finely chopped
1 Tbsp. chili powder
2 tsp. dried oregano
¼ tsp. ground cinnamon
1 15-oz. can pinto beans, drained and rinsed
½ cup defatted reduced-sodium chicken stock
2 cups prepared tomato salsa
¼ cup chopped fresh cilantro or parsley
salt & freshly ground black pepper to taste
8 corn tortillas
½ cup grated sharp Cheddar cheese

Preheat oven to 450 degrees F. Lightly oil an 8-by-11½-inch baking dish or coat it with nonstick cooking spray.

Heat a large nonstick skillet over medium-high heat. Add turkey; cook, stirring to break up meat, until no longer pink, about 5 minutes. Drain in a colander and set aside. Add oil to the skillet, then add onions and sauté until softened, 3 to 4 minutes. Add garlic, jalapeños, chili powder, oregano and cinnamon; sauté for 1 minute more. Mash beans coarsely and add to the skillet, along with chicken stock, 1 cup of the salsa and the reserved cooked turkey. Bring to a simmer and cook until thickened, about 5 minutes. Stir in cilantro or parsley and season with salt and pepper.

To assemble enchiladas, heat a tortilla directly on a hot stovetop burner, turning with tongs, until the tortilla is softened, about 30 seconds. Spoon about ½ cup of the turkey and bean filling down the center of the tortilla. Roll up and place seam-side-down in the prepared baking dish. Repeat with the remaining tortillas and filling. Spoon the remaining 1 cup salsa over the enchiladas and sprinkle with cheese. Bake for 10 minutes, or until heated through.

Serves 4.

549 CALORIES PER SERVING: 31 G PROTEIN, 18 G FAT, 71 G CARBOHYDRATE; 780 MG SODIUM; 62 MG CHOLESTEROL.

Jícama Slaw

¼ cup apple cider
1½ Tbsp. olive oil, preferably extra-virgin
1 Tbsp. cider vinegar
2 tsp. Dijon mustard
1 clove garlic, finely chopped
2 cups grated jícama (*see* "The Well-Stocked Kitchen" *on page 221*)
1 cup grated carrots
1 cup grated Granny Smith apples
  salt & freshly ground black pepper to taste

Timetable

1. Make strawberry-margarita ice.

2. Preheat oven to 450 degrees F.

3. Prepare and bake enchiladas.

4. Make slaw.

In a salad bowl, whisk apple cider, oil, vinegar, mustard and garlic. Add jícama, carrots and apples; toss to coat. Season with salt and pepper.

Makes about 4 cups.

Serves 4.

150 CALORIES PER SERVING: 1 G PROTEIN, 5 G FAT, 25 G CARBOHYDRATE; 26 MG SODIUM; 0 MG CHOLESTEROL.

Strawberry-Margarita Ice

12 oz. frozen whole strawberries

½ cup sugar, preferably superfine

¼ cup lime juice

2 Tbsp. tequila

1 Tbsp. Triple Sec or other orange liqueur

In a food processor, combine frozen strawberries and sugar. Using an on/off motion, process until coarsely chopped.

In a small bowl, stir together lime juice, tequila and Triple Sec. With machine running, gradually pour the mixture through the feed tube. Process until smooth and creamy, scraping down the sides of the bowl once or twice.

Scoop the mixture into chilled margarita glasses or individual serving dishes, cover with plastic wrap and freeze for 15 to 30 minutes to firm up slightly before serving.

Makes about 2 cups.

Serves 4.

145 CALORIES PER SERVING: 1 G PROTEIN, 0 G FAT, 33 G CARBOHYDRATE; 1 MG SODIUM; 0 MG CHOLESTEROL.

Lighthearted Chicken

In the entrée, tart apples and chicken breasts mingle in a sauce made fragrant by spices like ginger, coriander, cumin and mustard seeds. The ginger in the chicken dish is echoed by the ginger in the rice, which is also freshened with lemon juice and zest. Roasted green beans dotted with sesame seeds round out the menu. For dessert, we recommend sliced papaya. A ripe papaya is yellow and has a slight give to it, much like a ripe avocado; it is delicious sprinkled with fresh lime juice.

Apple-Ginger Chicken

2	cloves garlic, finely chopped
1	Tbsp. finely chopped fresh ginger
1	tsp. ground coriander
1	tsp. ground cumin
1	tsp. whole yellow mustard seeds
1	lb. boneless, skinless chicken breasts, fat trimmed, cut into ¼-inch-thick slices
1	Tbsp. all-purpose white flour
1½	tsp. vegetable oil, preferably canola oil
1	tart apple, such as Granny Smith, cored and cut into thin wedges
¾	cup defatted reduced-sodium chicken stock
	salt to taste
1	Tbsp. chopped fresh cilantro or parsley

In a small bowl, stir together garlic, ginger, coriander, cumin and mustard seeds; set aside.

In a medium-sized bowl, toss chicken with flour until evenly coated. In a large nonstick skillet or wok over high heat, heat 1 tsp. of the oil.

MENU

Apple-Ginger Chicken

Lemon Rice

Sesame Green Beans

(Sliced Papaya)

THIS MENU CONTAINS 519 CALORIES PER SERVING WITH 10% OF CALORIES FROM FAT.

Add the chicken and sauté until well-browned on all sides, about 4 minutes. With a slotted spoon, transfer the chicken to a plate and set aside.

Add the remaining ½ tsp. oil and apples to the pan. Reduce heat to medium and cook, stirring, until apples are lightly browned, about 3 minutes. Reduce heat to medium-low and add the reserved spice mixture. Stir until the apples are tender and the garlic is fragrant, 2 to 3 minutes. Add chicken stock and the reserved chicken; increase heat to high. Bring the mixture to a simmer and cook until the sauce is slightly thickened and the chicken is no longer pink inside, about 2 minutes. Season with salt. Transfer to a serving dish and sprinkle with cilantro or parsley.

Serves 4.

183 CALORIES PER SERVING: 27 G PROTEIN, 4 G FAT, 9 G CARBOHYDRATE; 76 MG SODIUM; 67 MG CHOLESTEROL.

Lemon Rice

1	onion, finely chopped
½	tsp. vegetable oil, preferably canola oil
1⅓	cups long-grain white rice
1	tsp. ground ginger
2½	cups defatted reduced-sodium chicken stock
¼	cup lemon juice
2	3-inch strips lemon zest
½	tsp. salt

Conventional Method: In a medium-sized saucepan, stir together onions and oil. Cover the pan and cook over low heat for 5 minutes. Add rice and ginger, raise heat to medium and cook, stirring, for 1 minute. Stir in chicken stock, lemon juice, lemon zest and salt; bring to a boil. Reduce heat to very low and cook, covered, until the liquid has been absorbed and the rice is tender, 15 to 17 minutes. Fluff with a fork before serving.

Microwave Method: In a microwave-safe 2½-qt. casserole, stir together onions and oil. Microwave on high power, uncovered, for 3 minutes, or until softened. Add rice, ginger, chicken stock, lemon juice, lemon zest and salt. Cover casserole with a lid or vented plastic wrap and microwave on high power for 5 to 7 minutes. Stir once, cover and microwave on medium power (50 percent), without stirring, for 17 to 20 minutes, or until rice is tender. Let stand, covered, for 5 minutes. Fluff with a fork before serving.

Serves 4.

257 CALORIES PER SERVING: 5 G PROTEIN, 1 G FAT, 55 G CARBOHYDRATE; 271 MG SODIUM; 1 MG CHOLESTEROL.

Sesame Green Beans

1 lb. green beans, trimmed
1 tsp. olive oil
2 tsp. sesame seeds
   salt & freshly ground black pepper to taste

Preheat oven to 450 degrees F. On a baking sheet with sides, toss beans with oil, then spread the beans out in a single layer. Roast the beans for about 12 minutes, stirring once, or until wrinkled, brown and tender.

In a small dry skillet over medium heat, stir sesame seeds until fragrant and toasted, about 1 minute. Crush the seeds lightly and toss with the beans. Season with salt and pepper.

Serves 4.

58 CALORIES PER SERVING: 2 G PROTEIN, 2 G FAT, 9 G CARBOHYDRATE; 4 MG SODIUM; 0 MG CHOLESTEROL.

A Pan-Roast with Pasta

For this easy pasta dish, there is no need to make a long-simmering sauce—it is all done in one pan in the oven in half an hour. Roasting deepens the flavor of the vegetables while keeping them distinct—particularly appealing if you have tired of blended tomato sauces—and it mellows the garlic into a sweet, unctuous paste. Roasting helps limit added fat as well: you need only drizzle two teaspoons of olive oil over the vegetables to keep them from sticking to the pan. A salad of crisp mixed greens provides a fresh contrast. For dessert, fresh berries are covered with a tangy low-fat cream, sprinkled with brown sugar and glazed under a hot broiler.

Fusilli with Roasted Shrimp, Tomatoes & Asparagus

- 12 plum tomatoes, cored and quartered lengthwise
- 4 tsp. olive oil, preferably extra-virgin
   freshly ground black pepper to taste
- 1 small head garlic
- 1 lb. thin asparagus, trimmed and cut into 2-inch lengths
   (or larger stalks, cut in half lengthwise before cutting)
- 1 lb. large shrimp, peeled and deveined
- ¾ lb. corkscrew pasta, such as fusilli or rotini
- 2 tsp. lemon juice
- 1 Tbsp. chopped fresh oregano or 1 tsp. dried
- 1 Tbsp. chopped fresh thyme or 1 tsp. dried thyme leaves
   salt to taste

Set oven rack in lower third of oven. Preheat oven to 450 degrees F.

In a large roasting pan, toss tomatoes with 2 tsp. of the olive oil and a generous grinding of pepper. Slice the top ½ inch off the garlic head and

MENU

....

*Fusilli with
Roasted Shrimp,
Tomatoes &
Asparagus*

*Tossed Salad
with Parmesan
Vinaigrette*

(French Bread)

*Fresh Berry
Gratin*

THIS MENU CONTAINS
892 CALORIES
PER SERVING WITH
23% OF CALORIES
FROM FAT.

1. *Preheat oven to 450 degrees F.*

2. *Wash salad greens.*

3. *Roast tomatoes and garlic.*

4. *Assemble berry gratin.*

5. *Heat water for pasta.*

6. *Add asparagus, shrimp to tomatoes.*

7. *Cook pasta.*

8. *Make salad dressing.*

9. *Finish pasta.*

10. *Preheat broiler for dessert.*

discard; pull off any loose papery skin. Wrap the garlic in aluminum foil and add to the roasting pan.

Roast for 20 to 30 minutes, without stirring, or until the tomatoes are wrinkled and beginning to brown. Scatter the asparagus and shrimp over the tomatoes and roast for 10 minutes more, or until the shrimp are curled and opaque in the center and the asparagus is tender. Remove the garlic from the pan, unwrap and let cool for 5 minutes. Cover the roasting pan to keep warm.

Meanwhile, in a large pot of boiling salted water, cook pasta until al dente, about 8 minutes. While the pasta is cooking, separate the garlic cloves and squeeze out the soft pulp. Mash to a paste with the flat side of a knife.

Drain the pasta and return to the pot. Add the remaining 2 tsp. olive oil, mashed garlic, lemon juice, oregano, thyme, salt and pepper, tossing to evenly coat the pasta with the seasonings. Transfer the pasta to the roasting pan and toss gently to combine, making sure to scrape up any bits that have adhered to the bottom of the pan.

Serves 4.

528 CALORIES PER SERVING: 39 G PROTEIN, 8 G FAT, 76 G CARBOHYDRATE; 276 MG SODIUM; 222 MG CHOLESTEROL.

Tossed Salad with Parmesan Vinaigrette

....

¼ cup freshly grated Parmesan cheese

2 Tbsp. white-wine vinegar

2 Tbsp. olive oil, preferably extra-virgin

2 Tbsp. strong brewed tea, such as Earl Grey or orange pekoe

½ tsp. finely chopped garlic

½ tsp. Dijon mustard

salt & freshly ground black pepper to taste

8 cups washed, dried and torn mixed greens

In a large salad bowl, whisk together Parmesan cheese, vinegar, oil, tea, garlic and mustard until well blended. Season with salt and pepper. Add greens and toss to combine.

Serves 4.

114 CALORIES PER SERVING: 6 G PROTEIN, 9 G FAT, 5 G CARBOHYDRATE; 206 MG SODIUM; 5 MG CHOLESTEROL.

Fresh Berry Gratin

3   cups fresh berries (raspberries, blueberries and/or blackberries)
4   oz. reduced-fat cream cheese, softened
3   Tbsp. skim milk
1   Tbsp. lemon juice
⅓   cup packed light brown sugar

Place berries in an even layer in a 9-inch pie plate or divide among 4 individual gratin dishes.

In a small bowl, whisk together cream cheese, milk and lemon juice. Spread over the berries, leaving the outer edge uncovered. Set aside in the refrigerator, covered with plastic wrap, for up to 1 hour.

Preheat the broiler. Press sugar through a coarse sieve over the berries, covering them evenly. Broil until the sugar has melted, about 4 minutes.

Serves 4.

178 CALORIES PER SERVING: 4 G PROTEIN, 6 G FAT, 31 G CARBOHYDRATE; 171 MG SODIUM; 10 MG CHOLESTEROL.

Quick Passage to India

MENU

....

*Pepper & Egg
Curry*

(Basmati Rice)

*Pineapple-Mint
Salad*

*Pistachio-Cardamom
Thins*

THIS MENU CONTAINS
540 CALORIES
PER SERVING WITH
26% OF CALORIES
FROM FAT.

This India-inspired menu features Pepper & Egg Curry served over fragrant basmati rice. Spicy but not overly hot, the main dish is a fun and different way to use eggs. Yogurt and lemon juice stirred in at the end give it a tangy smoothness that complements the heat of the curry powder, ginger and jalapeño peppers. Pineapple's season begins in spring (look for it already skinned and cored at the supermarket), and the cool and pretty salad in which it stars here is a refreshing break from the spicy curry. The Pistachio-Cardamom Thins are a twist on a French cookie with an Indian flavor. Surprisingly fast to mix up, they're a light, crisp way to end the meal.

Pepper & Egg Curry

- 4   large eggs
- 2   tsp. vegetable oil, preferably canola oil
- 1   onion, chopped
- 1   green bell pepper, cut into 1-inch dice
- 1   jalapeño pepper, seeded and finely chopped
- 2   tsp. finely chopped fresh ginger
- 2   Tbsp. all-purpose white flour
- 1   Tbsp. curry powder
- 1   tsp. ground cumin
- 2   cups defatted reduced-sodium chicken or vegetable stock
- ¼   cup nonfat plain yogurt
- 2   Tbsp. chopped fresh parsley
- 2   tsp. lemon juice

Place eggs in a medium-sized saucepan and cover with cold water. Bring to a simmer over medium heat and cook for 9 minutes. Remove from heat and pour off the hot water, holding back the eggs with a spoon; run under cold water, shaking the eggs to crack and loosen the shells. Peel and set aside to cool.

Heat oil in a large saucepan over medium heat. Add onions and green peppers and cook, stirring, until the onions begin to color, about 5 minutes. Add jalapeño peppers and ginger; stir for 1 minute. Stir in flour, curry powder and cumin and cook for 1 minute. Gradually whisk in chicken or vegetable stock; cook, stirring, until smooth and thickened, about 1 minute.

Remove the pan from the heat and whisk in yogurt, 1½ Tbsp. of the parsley and lemon juice. Cut the eggs into wedges and gently stir into the sauce. Sprinkle with the remaining ½ Tbsp. parsley and serve.

Serves 4.

177 CALORIES PER SERVING: 10 G PROTEIN, 8 G FAT, 15 G CARBOHYDRATE; 307 MG SODIUM; 220 MG CHOLESTEROL.

Pineapple-Mint Salad

2 cups diced fresh pineapple (½ pineapple)
¼ cup chopped red onion
2 Tbsp. chopped fresh mint
⅛ tsp. salt

Combine all ingredients in a small bowl.
Makes 2 cups.
Serves 4.

43 CALORIES PER SERVING: 0 G PROTEIN, 0 G FAT, 11 G CARBOHYDRATE; 69 MG SODIUM; 0 MG CHOLESTEROL.

Timetable

1. *Preheat oven to 300 degrees F.*

2. *Cook eggs for curry.*

3. *Mix and bake cookies.*

4. *Make pineapple salad.*

5. *Cook rice.*

6. *Make curry.*

Pistachio-Cardamom Thins

1 Tbsp. butter

2 Tbsp. chopped skinned pistachios, rinsed if salted

¼ cup sugar

3 Tbsp. all-purpose white flour

1 large egg white

pinch of ground cardamom or ginger

Preheat oven to 300 degrees F. Lightly oil a baking sheet or coat it with nonstick cooking spray.

In a small saucepan over medium heat, melt butter. Add pistachios and stir until the butter is lightly browned and the nuts are toasted, about 1 minute. Transfer the mixture to a medium-sized bowl. Whisk in sugar. Add flour, egg white and cardamom or ginger and whisk until smooth.

Drop the batter by heaping teaspoonfuls, about 2 inches apart, onto the prepared baking sheet. Bake for 12 to 15 minutes, or until golden. With a spatula, immediately transfer the cookies to a rack to cool. (If the cookies begin to stick before all are removed, return the pan briefly to the oven.)

Makes 1 dozen cookies.

40 CALORIES PER COOKIE: 1 G PROTEIN, 2 G FAT, 6 G CARBOHYDRATE; 14 MG SODIUM; 3 MG CHOLESTEROL.

Fast Soup from the Far East

This Chinese-inspired seafood-and-noodle soup is best eaten with chopsticks and a spoon. The pale, subtle colors and flavors of the scallops, shrimp, noodles and Napa cabbage in the soup are balanced by the crunchy broccoli and red bell peppers in the salad, dressed with a sweet-spicy vinegar-and-oil mix. The fruit compote's delicate flavors and colors are a serene, cool way to end the meal; serve with store-bought fortune cookies for a bit of fun and crunch.

Chinese Seafood Soup

1	tsp. vegetable oil, preferably canola oil
3	cloves garlic, finely chopped
3	cups thinly sliced Napa (Chinese) cabbage (½ of a small head)
4	cups defatted reduced-sodium chicken stock
6	oz. small shrimp, peeled and deveined
6	oz. scallops, cut in half crosswise
3	Tbsp. reduced-sodium soy sauce
2	Tbsp. rice-wine vinegar
½	lb. Chinese wheat noodles or linguine
2	scallions, trimmed and chopped

In a medium-sized saucepan, heat oil over medium heat. Add garlic and stir until golden, about 1 minute. Add cabbage and ¼ cup of the chicken stock. Bring to a simmer and cook until the cabbage is wilted, about 1 minute. Add remaining chicken stock, shrimp, scallops, soy sauce and vinegar. Return to a simmer and cook until the seafood is opaque in the center, about 1 minute.

Meanwhile, in a large pot of boiling salted water, cook noodles just

THIS MENU CONTAINS 565 CALORIES PER SERVING WITH 15% OF CALORIES FROM FAT.

....

1. *Steam broccoli and make dressing.*

2. *Toast coconut for compote.*

3. *Heat water for noodles.*

4. *Prepare soup ingredients.*

5. *Make fruit compote.*

6. *Make soup.*

7. *Toss salad.*

until tender, 2 to 5 minutes. If using linguine, cook until al dente, 8 to 10 minutes. Drain in a colander and divide among 4 large soup bowls.

Ladle the soup over the noodles and sprinkle with scallions.

Serves 4.

315 CALORIES PER SERVING: 24 G PROTEIN, 3 G FAT, 46 G CARBOHYDRATE; 2,571 MG SODIUM; 80 MG CHOLESTEROL.

Spicy Broccoli Salad

1½	lbs. broccoli
3	Tbsp. chopped red bell pepper
3	Tbsp. chopped red onion
3	Tbsp. rice-wine vinegar
1	Tbsp. sesame oil
2	tsp. light brown sugar
1	tsp. red-pepper flakes
	salt to taste

Cut off broccoli florets. Trim and peel stems; cut into ½-inch-thick slices. Place broccoli florets and stems in a steamer basket over boiling water; cover and steam for 2 to 3 minutes, or until crisp-tender. Refresh under cold water. Drain well.

In a medium-sized bowl, stir together red peppers, onions, vinegar, oil, brown sugar and red-pepper flakes. Just before serving, add the broccoli and toss to combine. Season with salt.

Serves 4.

101 CALORIES PER SERVING: 6 G PROTEIN, 4 G FAT, 14 G CARBOHYDRATE; 233 MG SODIUM; 0 MG CHOLESTEROL.

Fruit Compote with Coconut

2   Tbsp. sweetened shredded coconut

½   pt. strawberries, hulled and sliced

1   cup cantaloupe balls or cubes (½ cantaloupe)

2   kiwi fruit, peeled, cut in half and sliced

¼   cup orange juice

2   Tbsp. chopped crystallized ginger or preserved stem ginger

2   tsp. sugar

In a small dry skillet over medium heat, stir coconut until lightly toasted, about 1 minute. Transfer to a plate to cool.

In a medium-sized bowl, combine strawberries, cantaloupe, kiwi fruit, orange juice, ginger and sugar. Stir gently. Serve in individual bowls, sprinkled with toasted coconut.

Serves 4.

119 CALORIES PER SERVING: 1 G PROTEIN, 3 G FAT, 24 G CARBOHYDRATE; 36 MG SODIUM; 0 MG CHOLESTEROL.

Pasta & Tomato Sauce I

Lemon peel gives this tomato-based sauce a slightly bitter-tart tang that highlights the meaty chunks of fresh tuna. For a vivid flavor accent, *gremolata*, an Italian mixture of parsley, garlic and lemon zest, is dusted over the top just before serving. Roasting is a wonderful way to cook asparagus. Not only simple and fast, it intensifies the taste, which the slightly sweet balsamic vinegar sharpens. Rhubarb, a classic spring flavor, is paired with orange to mellow it a bit in our dessert offering for this low-fat menu.

Fettuccine with Fresh Tuna Sauce

3 tsp. olive oil
¾ lb. fresh tuna steak (1 inch thick), cut into 1-inch cubes
   salt & freshly ground black pepper to taste
1 onion, chopped
1 carrot, chopped
1 stalk celery, chopped
4 tsp. finely chopped garlic (4 cloves)
1 28-oz. can plum tomatoes, with juices
¾ cup defatted reduced-sodium chicken stock
¾ cup dry white wine
¼ tsp. dried thyme leaves
2 strips lemon zest plus 1 Tbsp. grated
1 bay leaf
3 Tbsp. chopped fresh parsley
¾ lb. fettuccine or linguine

In a large nonstick skillet, heat 1½ tsp. of the oil over medium-high heat. Add tuna and sauté until browned on the outside but still pink inside,

Timetable

1. *Preheat oven to 450 degrees F.*

2. *Make stewed rhubarb.*

3. *Heat water for pasta.*

4. *Make tuna sauce and topping.*

5. *Prepare and roast asparagus.*

6. *Cook pasta.*

about 2 minutes. Remove from the skillet, season with salt and pepper and set aside.

Reduce heat to medium and add the remaining 1½ tsp. of the oil to the skillet. Add onions, carrots, celery and 3 tsp. of the chopped garlic. Sauté until the vegetables are softened, about 3 minutes. Add tomatoes and mash with the back of a spoon or a potato masher. Add stock, wine, thyme, strips of lemon zest and bay leaf; bring to a boil over medium-high heat. Cook until slightly thickened, about 15 minutes.

Return the tuna to the sauce, reduce heat to low and simmer, stirring occasionally, until the fish is opaque in the center, about 5 minutes more. Discard strips of lemon zest and bay leaf. Taste and adjust seasonings.

Meanwhile, in a small bowl, combine parsley, grated lemon zest and the remaining 1 tsp. chopped garlic; set aside.

Cook fettuccine or linguine in a large pot of boiling salted water until al dente, 8 to 10 minutes. Drain and place on individual plates. Spoon the tuna sauce over the top. Sprinkle with the parsley mixture and serve.

Serves 4.

539 CALORIES PER SERVING: 34 G PROTEIN, 6 G FAT, 80 G CARBOHYDRATE; 524 MG SODIUM; 38 MG CHOLESTEROL.

Roasted Asparagus

1½	lbs. asparagus
2	tsp. olive oil
	salt & freshly ground black pepper to taste
1	tsp. balsamic vinegar

Preheat oven to 450 degrees F. Snap off the tough ends of asparagus and, if desired, peel the stalks.

In a shallow roasting pan or baking sheet with sides, toss the asparagus with oil and season with salt and pepper. Spread the asparagus in a single layer.

Roast for 10 to 15 minutes, or until tender and browned, shaking once during roasting. Sprinkle with balsamic vinegar and toss. Taste and adjust seasonings.

Serves 4.

64 CALORIES PER SERVING: 4 G PROTEIN, 3 G FAT, 8 G CARBOHYDRATE; 7 MG SODIUM; 0 MG CHOLESTEROL.

Stewed Rhubarb with Orange

1 lb. rhubarb, trimmed and cut into 1-inch pieces (4 cups)
½ cup orange marmalade
¼ cup sugar
⅛ tsp. ground cinnamon
⅛ tsp. freshly grated nutmeg

In a medium-sized saucepan, stir together rhubarb, marmalade, sugar, cinnamon, nutmeg and 2 Tbsp. water. Bring to a simmer, reduce heat to low and cover the pan. Cook, stirring occasionally, until the rhubarb is tender, 6 to 8 minutes. (*Alternatively, microwave, covered, on high power for 6 to 7 minutes, stirring midway. Let stand, covered, for 5 minutes.*)

Serves 4.

180 CALORIES PER SERVING: 1 G PROTEIN, 0 G FAT, 45 G CARBOHYDRATE; 9 MG SODIUM; 0 MG CHOLESTEROL.

Dinner at the Oasis

MENU

....

Vegetable Tagine
with Couscous

Romaine &
Fresh Herb Salad

Apricot Whip
with Raspberries

THIS MENU CONTAINS
826 CALORIES
PER SERVING WITH
19% OF CALORIES
FROM FAT.

Moroccan tagines—rich, colorful stews—take their names from the clay vessels in which they are traditionally cooked, but they also can be successfully prepared in large pots. This flavorful tagine blends lots of fresh vegetables with chickpeas, sweet raisins and crunchy whole almonds. The romaine salad, brightened with the fresh herbs, is a simple counterpoint to the tagine's complexity. Apricots and other dried fruits often star in Moroccan desserts; this creamy version combines them with orange juice, brandy or vanilla and yogurt. Rich and fat-free, the puree's pale apricot color is accented by the deep red raspberries.

Vegetable Tagine with Couscous

3 tsp. olive oil

1 onion, finely chopped

2 cloves garlic, sliced

1 14-oz. can whole tomatoes, drained and chopped

2 cups defatted reduced-sodium chicken or vegetable stock

¼ cup whole blanched almonds

⅓ cup raisins

2 tsp. ground ginger

2 tsp. paprika

1 tsp. ground cinnamon

¼ tsp. saffron threads or pinch of powdered saffron (optional)

6 oz. green beans, ends trimmed, cut into 2-inch lengths

2 carrots, peeled and cut into ⅛-inch-thick slices

1 15-oz. can chickpeas, drained and rinsed

1 red bell pepper, cored, seeded and cut into 1-inch pieces

1½ cups couscous, preferably whole-wheat
½ tsp. salt
1½ Tbsp. lemon juice
2 tsp. harissa or Chinese chili paste (*see* "The Well-Stocked Kitchen" *on page 221*)
freshly ground black pepper to taste

In a soup pot, heat 2 tsp. of the oil over medium heat. Add onions and garlic and cook until golden, 3 to 5 minutes. Stir in tomatoes, stock, almonds, raisins, ginger, paprika, cinnamon and saffron (if using); bring to a boil. Add beans and carrots; return to a boil. Reduce heat to low, cover and simmer for 10 minutes. Mix in chickpeas and peppers; cook, covered, until the vegetables are tender, 7 to 10 minutes.

Meanwhile, in a large saucepan, bring 2¼ cups water to a boil. Stir in couscous, salt and the remaining 1 tsp. oil. Remove from the heat, cover and let stand for 5 minutes. Fluff with a fork.

Just before serving, stir lemon juice and harissa or chili paste into the stew. Season with pepper and serve over the couscous.

Serves 4.

600 CALORIES PER SERVING: 20 G PROTEIN, 13 G FAT, 108 G CARBOHYDRATE; 903 MG SODIUM; 1 MG CHOLESTEROL.

Romaine & Fresh Herb Salad

1 clove garlic, cut in half
6 cups washed, dried and torn romaine lettuce (1 head)
⅓ cup finely chopped fresh parsley
2 Tbsp. chopped fresh chives or scallions
2 Tbsp. finely chopped fresh dill
1 Tbsp. finely chopped fresh mint
1½ Tbsp. balsamic vinegar or lemon juice
1 Tbsp. olive oil, preferably extra-virgin
salt & freshly ground black pepper to taste

Timetable

1. *Simmer apricots for dessert.*

2. *Prepare salad greens and herbs.*

3. *Make salad dressing.*

4. *Finish dessert.*

5. *Make vegetable tagine.*

6. *Make couscous.*

Rub a large salad bowl with the cut sides of garlic. Place romaine, parsley, chives or scallions, dill and mint in the bowl.

In a small bowl or jar, mix together vinegar or lemon juice, oil, salt and pepper. Drizzle the dressing over the salad, toss and serve.

Serves 4.

56 CALORIES PER SERVING: 2 G PROTEIN, 4 G FAT, 5 G CARBOHYDRATE; 13 MG SODIUM; 0 MG CHOLESTEROL.

Apricot Whip with Raspberries

½ cup firmly packed dried apricots

½ cup orange juice

¼ cup sugar

2 Tbsp. brandy or 1 tsp. pure vanilla extract

1½ cups nonfat plain yogurt

½ cup fresh raspberries or frozen raspberries, thawed

In a medium-sized saucepan, combine apricots, orange juice and sugar. Bring the mixture to a boil; reduce heat to low and simmer gently until the apricots are tender, about 12 minutes.

Transfer the apricots and cooking liquid to a blender or food processor, add brandy or vanilla and puree. Transfer to a medium-sized bowl and stir in yogurt. Chill until serving time. Serve topped with raspberries.

Serves 4.

170 CALORIES PER SERVING: 6 G PROTEIN, 0 G FAT, 34 G CARBOHYDRATE; 67 MG SODIUM; 2 MG CHOLESTEROL.

Spring Frittata

A casual frittata turns a handful of asparagus spears into supper. There's no meat in this light egg dish, made lighter still because egg whites replace some of the whole eggs. The Chickpea & Red Onion Salad is tart with lemon juice and capers. For dessert, quick Strawberry Shortcakes are made with store-bought fat-free pound cake. The low-fat vanilla yogurt topping is a fast and rich-tasting alternative to whipped cream. This dish would also be delicious with raspberries or cherries.

Asparagus Frittata

2	small potatoes, cut into ½-inch dice
10-12	asparagus spears, cut into 2-inch pieces
3	tsp. vegetable oil, preferably canola oil
1	small onion, thinly sliced
1	clove garlic, finely chopped
1	tsp. chopped fresh rosemary or ½ tsp. dried
1	tomato, cored, seeded and chopped
½	tsp. salt
½	tsp. freshly ground black pepper, plus more to taste
4	large eggs
4	large egg whites
¼	cup freshly grated Parmesan or Gruyère cheese
	fresh chives for garnish

Conventional Method: Place potatoes in a steamer basket over boiling water; cover and cook for 4 minutes. Add asparagus and cook until the vegetables are tender, 2 to 3 minutes more. **Microwave Method:** Place asparagus in the center of a large microwave-safe platter. Arrange a ring

MENU
....

Asparagus Frittata

*Chickpea &
Red Onion Salad*

(Italian Bread)

*Strawberry
Shortcakes*

THIS MENU CONTAINS
825 CALORIES
PER SERVING WITH
27% OF CALORIES
FROM FAT.

of potatoes around the asparagus. Add ¼ cup water, cover with a lid or vented plastic wrap and microwave on high power for 4 to 6 minutes, or until vegetables are just tender. Drain.

Transfer the potatoes and asparagus to a bowl to cool.

Preheat the broiler. Heat 2 tsp. of the oil in a large, ovenproof, non-stick skillet over medium heat. Add onions, garlic, rosemary and half of the tomatoes. Cook, stirring, until the onions are limp, about 8 minutes. Add the mixture to the reserved potatoes and asparagus, season with salt and pepper and set aside.

Wipe out the skillet and brush with the remaining 1 tsp. oil. Return the skillet to low heat. In a medium-sized bowl, lightly whisk together whole eggs, egg whites and Parmesan or Gruyère. Add the vegetables to the egg mixture and pour into the skillet, gently stirring to distribute the vegetables. Cook over low heat until the underside is light golden, 5 to 8 minutes.

Place the skillet under the broiler and broil until the top of the frittata is puffed and golden brown, 1 to 2 minutes. Loosen the frittata and slide onto a platter. Garnish with chives and the remaining chopped tomatoes.

Serves 4.

225 CALORIES PER SERVING: 14 G PROTEIN, 11 G FAT, 19 G CARBOHYDRATE; 508 MG SODIUM; 218 MG CHOLESTEROL.

Chickpea & Red Onion Salad

nice protein salad

¼ cup slivered red onion
1 19-oz. can chickpeas, drained and rinsed
½ cup chopped fresh parsley
2 Tbsp. lemon juice
1 Tbsp. olive oil, preferably extra-virgin
1 Tbsp. drained capers, rinsed and coarsely chopped
    salt & freshly ground black pepper to taste
    red leaf lettuce leaves

Timetable

1. *Drain yogurt for shortcake.*

2. *Cook potatoes and asparagus for frittata.*

3. *Soak onions for salad.*

4. *Slice berries; toss with sugar.*

5. *Preheat broiler.*

6. *Finish salad.*

7. *Make frittata.*

In a medium-sized bowl, cover onions with cold water and let soak for 10 minutes. Drain well and place in a salad bowl. Add chickpeas, parsley, lemon juice, oil and capers; stir to combine. Season with salt and pepper. Serve on lettuce leaves.

Makes 2¼ cups.

Serves 4.

156 CALORIES PER SERVING: 6 G PROTEIN, 6 G FAT, 22 G CARBOHYDRATE; 563 MG SODIUM; 0 MG CHOLESTEROL.

Strawberry Shortcakes

1   cup low-fat vanilla yogurt
1   pt. strawberries, hulled and sliced
3   Tbsp. sugar
4   slices fat-free pound cake (6 oz. total)

Line a sieve with cheesecloth and set it over a bowl. (*Alternatively, line a coffee filter with filter paper.*) Spoon in yogurt and let drain in the refrigerator for 30 to 60 minutes.

In a medium-sized bowl, toss strawberries with sugar. Let stand at room temperature for about 30 minutes, stirring occasionally, until a syrup has formed.

Place pound cake slices on dessert plates. Spoon the strawberries and syrup over the cake and add a dollop of the drained yogurt.

Serves 4.

304 CALORIES PER SERVING: 5 G PROTEIN, 8 G FAT, 54 G CARBOHYDRATE; 209 MG SODIUM; 4 MG CHOLESTEROL.

Bowlful of Fragrant Mussels

This seafood classic is nearly an instant supper. First, there's a bountiful bowl of fragrant mussels swimming in a garlicky white wine and tomato broth. Served alongside is a bright lemony mayonnaise that features watercress and scallions. Spread it on warm French bread or spoon some on the mussels. And maple, which signals the arrival of spring (that's when the trees are tapped for their running sap), is used here in a smooth and rich-tasting custard.

Steamed Mussels in Tomato Broth

1   tsp. olive oil
4   cloves garlic, finely chopped
6   ripe plum tomatoes, cored and coarsely chopped
1   cup dry white wine
3   lbs. mussels, scrubbed and debearded
2   tsp. chopped fresh parsley

In a large pot with a tight-fitting lid, warm oil over low heat. Add garlic and cook, stirring, until golden, about 3 minutes. Add tomatoes, increase heat to high and stir for 1 minute more. Add wine and bring to a boil. Add mussels, cover the pan and steam, occasionally giving the pan a vigorous shake, until all the mussels have opened, 3 to 4 minutes. Discard any that do not open. Transfer the mussels to a large serving bowl. Slowly pour the broth over them, leaving behind any sand in the pot. Sprinkle with parsley.

Serves 4.

270 CALORIES PER SERVING: 28 G PROTEIN, 7 G FAT, 14 G CARBOHYDRATE; 430 MG SODIUM; 64 MG CHOLESTEROL.

Timetable

....

1. *Preheat oven to 325 degrees F.*

2. *Prepare and bake custards.*

3. *Make herb sauce.*

4. *Clean and steam mussels.*

Herb Sauce

⅓ cup finely chopped watercress leaves
¼ cup reduced-fat mayonnaise
2 Tbsp. finely chopped scallions
1 Tbsp. olive oil, preferably extra-virgin
1 Tbsp. lemon juice
1 clove garlic, finely chopped
½ tsp. grated lemon zest
   salt & freshly ground black pepper to taste

In a small bowl, stir together watercress, mayonnaise, scallions, olive oil, lemon juice, garlic and lemon zest until creamy. Season with salt and pepper. Serve with French bread.
   Makes about ½ cup.
   Serves 4.

73 CALORIES PER SERVING: 0 G PROTEIN, 7 G FAT, 2 G CARBOHYDRATE; 1 MG SODIUM; 5 MG CHOLESTEROL.

Maple Custards

½ cup maple syrup, plus 4 tsp. for topping
¾ cup skim milk
⅔ cup evaporated skim milk
2 large eggs
2 large egg yolks

Conventional Method: Preheat oven to 325 degrees F. In a medium-sized saucepan over high heat, bring ½ cup maple syrup to a boil. Cook until thickened and reduced to about ¼ cup, about 4 minutes. Reduce heat to low and add skim milk and evaporated skim milk. Stir until the syrup has completely blended with the milk. Remove from heat.

In a medium-sized bowl, lightly whisk eggs and egg yolks until well combined. Gradually whisk the hot milk mixture into the eggs. Skim off any foam and divide the mixture among four 6-oz. custard cups. Place in a shallow baking dish and add enough hot water to come two-thirds up the sides of the cups. Bake for 30 to 40 minutes, or until a knife inserted in the center of the custard comes out clean.

Microwave Method: Follow above method up through pouring custard into cups. Place on a large plate, 1 inch apart. Microwave, uncovered, on medium power (50 percent) for 3 minutes; rotate 90 degrees and microwave for 2 minutes more. Check for doneness; custard should be well set 1 inch in from the edge and softly set in the center. Remove any custards as they are done; continue microwaving the remaining custards, checking for doneness every 30 seconds.

Transfer to a rack to cool until serving time. Serve warm, drizzled with remaining maple syrup.

Serves 4.

245 CALORIES PER SERVING: 9 G PROTEIN, 5 G FAT, 42 G CARBOHYDRATE; 155 MG SODIUM; 216 MG CHOLESTEROL.

Summer Menus

A Classic Summer Supper - 65

Barbecued Chicken • Tricolor Coleslaw • Grilled Corn on the Cob
Peach-Melon Frozen Yogurt

Jazzy, Fizzy, Fun & Fast - 68

Linguine with Tomato-Mint Sauce • (Italian Bread)
Spinach Salad with Black Olive Vinaigrette • Summer Berry Fizz

Hot Tuna, Cold Noodles - 71

Tuna with Scallion-Ginger Relish • Cold Soba or Somen Noodles
Watercress Salad • (Raspberries & Mangoes)

One from the Lime Latitudes - 75

Chicken Yucatan • Caribbean Rice & Beans • (Sliced Tomatoes)
(Warm Corn Tortillas) • Broiled Pineapple

Grillwork - 78

Swordfish Kebabs • Bruschetta with Tomatoes • Grilled Red Onions
Black Fruit Compote

Rebirth of the Burger - 81

Chili Burgers • Herbed Potato Salad • Blueberry-Lime Yogurt

An Hour in Provence - 85

Pan Bagna • Romaine Salad with Garlic Dressing • Peach Compote with Basil

Our Idea of Finger Food - 88

Zucchini & Carrot Sticks with Black-Eyed Pea Dip • Grilled Orange Chicken Fingers
Penne & Roasted Pepper Salad • Summer Blackberries

One Arabian Night - 92

Eggplant-Couscous Rolls • Carrot Salad with Cumin • (Pita Bread) • Gingered Peach Gratin

The Magic of Fish & Ginger - 96

Salmon in a Vibrant Sauce • Swiss Chard & Sweet Pepper Stir-Fry • (Basmati Rice)
Strawberries with Minted Yogurt

Chicken Wearing a Bow Tie - 99

Chicken & Bow Ties Salad • Snow Peas with Orange • Vanilla Nectarines

Salad to Start, Soup to Finish - 102

Grilled Sirloin Salad • Tomato-Garlic Toasts • Cold Plum Soup

Presto! Penne & Peas - 106

Penne with Sugar Snap Peas • Marinated Carrots • Lemon Frozen Yogurt with Berries

Seoul Supper - 109

Korean Shrimp Pancakes • Sticky Rice with Peas • (Kimchee)
Strawberries with Ginger & Pine Nuts

Salad on the Grill - 112

Grilled Mediterranean Vegetable Salad • Garlic Croutons
Macedoine of Melon & Hazelnuts with Ouzo • (Anisette Toasts)

A Classic Summer Supper

The days are long, it's time to enjoy the simple pleasure of cooking outdoors and eating relaxed meals on the deck. A down-home, all-American meal is in order: barbecued chicken, grilled corn on the cob and slaw, followed by a frozen fruit dessert, fits the bill. The barbecue sauce for the chicken relies on a combination of Asian condiments (all available at most supermarkets) quickly blended with ketchup and cider vinegar for a tomatoey pungency. Basting the chicken with the sauce throughout grilling gives the meat a crisp glaze. Briefly soaked in cold water, the corn steams in its husk alongside. Red and green cabbage and bright orange carrots make a colorful, healthful combination in Tricolor Coleslaw. For Peach-Melon Frozen Yogurt, start with frozen fruit and you'll have a delicious, fresh-tasting dessert five minutes later; strawberries, bananas and blueberries (alone or as a combination) are delicious, but avoid seedy fruits, such as raspberries.

Barbecued Chicken

1	3-lb. chicken, cut into 8 pieces, skin and fat removed
⅓	cup tomato ketchup
¼	cup hoisin sauce
1	Tbsp. cider vinegar
1	Tbsp. molasses
1	tsp. reduced-sodium soy sauce
1	tsp. Chinese chili paste with garlic

Arrange chicken pieces in a large microwaveable dish with the thickest parts toward the outside of the dish. Cover with vented plastic wrap and microwave at high power for 8 to 10 minutes, turning the chicken pieces

MENU

....

Barbecued Chicken

Tricolor Coleslaw

Grilled Corn on the Cob

Peach-Melon Frozen Yogurt

THIS MENU CONTAINS 694 CALORIES PER SERVING WITH 23% OF CALORIES FROM FAT.

Timetable

....

1. *Make peach-melon frozen yogurt.*

2. *Make coleslaw.*

3. *Preheat grill.*

4. *Prepare corn and soak.*

5. *Precook chicken.*

6. *Make barbecue sauce.*

7. *Grill corn and chicken.*

twice, or until tender. (*Alternatively, in a wide saucepan, cover chicken with cold water and bring to a simmer, skimming off any foam. Simmer gently until the chicken is tender, 10 to 12 minutes.*)

Meanwhile, prepare a grill. In a small bowl, whisk together ketchup, hoisin sauce, vinegar, molasses, soy sauce and chili paste.

With tongs, remove the chicken from the dish or saucepan and brush both sides generously with barbecue sauce.

Lightly oil the grill rack. Grill the chicken over medium-high heat, basting often with the barbecue sauce, until the meat is glazed on the outside and no longer pink inside, about 5 minutes on each side.

Serves 4.

376 CALORIES PER SERVING: 50 G PROTEIN, 13 G FAT, 13 G CARBOHYDRATE; 485 MG SODIUM; 152 MG CHOLESTEROL.

Tricolor Coleslaw

....

3 Tbsp. reduced-fat mayonnaise

3 Tbsp. nonfat plain yogurt

1 Tbsp. Dijon mustard

2 tsp. cider vinegar

1 tsp. sugar

½ tsp. caraway seeds (optional)

   salt & freshly ground black pepper to taste

2 cups shredded red cabbage (¼ of a small head)

2 cups shredded green cabbage, preferably Savoy (¼ of a small head)

1 cup grated carrots (2 medium carrots)

In a large bowl, combine mayonnaise, yogurt, mustard, vinegar, sugar and caraway seeds, if using. Season with salt and pepper. Add red and green cabbage and carrots and toss well.

Serves 4.

70 CALORIES PER SERVING: 2 G PROTEIN, 3 G FAT, 10 G CARBOHYDRATE; 37 MG SODIUM; 4 MG CHOLESTEROL.

Grilled Corn on the Cob

4 **ears of corn, unhusked**

Prepare a grill. Carefully peel back husks but do not detach. Remove as much silk as possible. Pull the husks back over the corn and secure the end by tying with a strip of husk. Soak the corn in cold water for 20 minutes. Remove from the water, shaking off excess.

Grill the ears of corn, periodically rolling them for even cooking, until the kernels are tender when pierced with a fork, 15 to 20 minutes. Remove the husks before serving.

Serves 4.

118 CALORIES PER SERVING: 4 G PROTEIN, 1 G FAT, 28 G CARBOHYDRATE; 6 MG SODIUM; 0 MG CHOLESTEROL.

Peach-Melon Frozen Yogurt

3 **cups frozen mixed fruit (peaches, melon, grapes)**
⅓ **cup sugar, preferably superfine**
½ **cup nonfat plain yogurt**
1 **Tbsp. lemon juice**

In a food processor, combine frozen fruit and sugar. Using an on/off motion, process until coarsely chopped.

In a small bowl, stir together yogurt and lemon juice. With the machine running, gradually pour the yogurt mixture through the feed tube. Process until smooth and creamy, scraping down the sides of the work bowl once or twice.

Scoop the frozen yogurt into serving dishes, cover with plastic wrap and freeze for at least 15 to 30 minutes to firm up before serving.

Serves 4.

119 CALORIES PER SERVING: 3 G PROTEIN, 0 G FAT, 29 G CARBOHYDRATE; 62 MG SODIUM; 1 MG CHOLESTEROL.

Jazzy, Fizzy, Fun & Fast

MENU

....

*Linguine
with Tomato-
Mint Sauce*

(Italian Bread)

*Spinach Salad
with Black Olive
Vinaigrette*

*Summer
Berry Fizz*

THIS MENU CONTAINS
917 CALORIES
PER SERVING WITH
9% OF CALORIES
FROM FAT.

How to jazz up a jar of commercial spaghetti sauce? Freshen it with ripe summer tomatoes, a couple of cloves of garlic, chopped fresh herbs and a brightening touch of lemon. You wind up with the complexity of a slow-cooked sauce spiked with the vibrant notes of fresh tomatoes. The spinach salad is a pleasing counterpoint to the main course; choose a top-flight virgin olive oil to bring out the flavors in the black-olive vinaigrette. Dessert is amusing—an old-fashioned soda for grown-ups. Chilled club soda is flavored with berry liqueur or brandy and topped with a scoop of fruit sorbet. Fizzy, fun and best eaten with a spoon and a straw.

Linguine with Tomato-Mint Sauce

1 lb. linguine
2 tsp. olive oil
2 cloves garlic, finely chopped
2 vine-ripened tomatoes, cored and chopped
1 tsp. lemon juice
2 cups spaghetti sauce
½ cup chopped fresh parsley
¼ cup chopped fresh mint
   salt & freshly ground black pepper to taste

In a large pot of boiling salted water, cook linguine until al dente, 8 to 10 minutes.

   Meanwhile, in a large nonstick skillet, heat oil over medium heat. Add garlic and cook, stirring, until softened, about 1 minute. Add tomatoes and lemon juice and cook for 1 minute more. Add spaghetti sauce, bring to a simmer and cook for 5 minutes. Remove from heat; stir in parsley and mint. Season with salt and pepper. Drain the pasta and serve topped with sauce.

Serves 4.

504 CALORIES PER SERVING: 17 G PROTEIN, 4 G FAT, 98 G CARBOHYDRATE; 52 MG SODIUM; 0 MG CHOLESTEROL.

Spinach Salad with Black Olive Vinaigrette

6	imported black olives, preferably Kalamata, pitted and finely chopped
1½	Tbsp. red-wine vinegar or lemon juice
1½	Tbsp. olive oil, preferably extra-virgin
1	Tbsp. defatted reduced-sodium chicken stock
¼	tsp. sugar
	salt & freshly ground black pepper to taste
6	cups washed, dried and torn spinach leaves (6 oz.)
½	cucumber, seeded and sliced
½	red onion, thinly sliced

In a salad bowl, whisk together olives, vinegar, olive oil, chicken stock and sugar. Season with salt and pepper. Add spinach, cucumbers and onions; toss well.

Serves 4.

57 CALORIES PER SERVING: 2 G PROTEIN, 4 G FAT, 5 G CARBOHYDRATE; 83 MG SODIUM; 0 MG CHOLESTEROL.

Timetable

1. *Heat water for pasta.*

2. *Clean spinach; slice salad vegetables.*

3. *Make salad dressing.*

4. *Cook pasta.*

5. *Make pasta sauce.*

Summer Berry Fizz

12 Tbsp. Chambord, crème de cassis or other berry-flavored liqueur or brandy

2 tsp. balsamic vinegar (optional)

3 cups chilled club soda

1 pt. raspberry or strawberry sorbet

In each of 4 tall glasses, stir together 3 Tbsp. liqueur or brandy and ½ tsp. vinegar, if using. Stir in ¾ cup club soda and top with ½ cup sorbet. Serves 4.

208 CALORIES PER SERVING: 1 G PROTEIN, 0 G FAT, 32 G CARBOHYDRATE; 44 MG SODIUM; 0 MG CHOLESTEROL.

Hot Tuna, Cold Noodles

With its dense, firm flesh, tuna is a great choice for the grill, but take care not to overcook it, as it can become dry. We've given the fish an Asian flavor here by accenting it with a sweet-and-sour scallion-ginger relish. Serve the tuna on a cool bed of Japanese noodles. The buckwheat flour in soba gives these noodles an earthy, rounded flavor; somen are fine white wheat noodles. A simple, sharp salad of watercress in a sesame-oil dressing completes the main course. Sliced fresh mangoes and a handful of raspberries are all you need for dessert.

Tuna with Scallion-Ginger Relish

SCALLION-GINGER RELISH

- 1 Tbsp. sesame seeds
- 1 cup thinly sliced scallions
- ¼ cup drained, canned water chestnuts, sliced
- 2 Tbsp. reduced-sodium soy sauce
- 2 Tbsp. orange juice
- 2 Tbsp. rice-wine vinegar
- 1 Tbsp. finely chopped fresh ginger
- 2 tsp. sugar
- 1 tsp. Chinese chili paste (*see* "The Well-Stocked Kitchen" *on page 221*) or hot sauce
  freshly ground white or black pepper to taste

TUNA

- 2 8-oz. tuna steaks, about 1 inch thick
- ½ tsp. vegetable oil, preferably canola oil
  salt & freshly ground black pepper to taste

THIS MENU CONTAINS 537 CALORIES PER SERVING WITH 22% OF CALORIES FROM FAT.

1. *Preheat grill.*

2. *Heat water for noodles.*

3. *Cook noodles.*

4. *Make scallion-ginger relish.*

5. *Wash watercress; make dressing.*

6. *Grill tuna.*

To prepare relish: In a small dry skillet over medium-high heat, stir sesame seeds until lightly toasted, 2 to 3 minutes.

In a small bowl, combine the sesame seeds with scallions, water chestnuts, soy sauce, orange juice, vinegar, ginger, sugar and chili paste or hot sauce. Season with pepper and toss well.

To grill tuna: Prepare a grill. Rub tuna steaks lightly with oil and sprinkle with salt and pepper. Grill the steaks, turning once, until the flesh is opaque in the center, 4 to 5 minutes per side.

Divide each steak into 2 portions and serve topped with the relish.
Serves 4.

203 CALORIES PER SERVING: 28 G PROTEIN, 7 G FAT, 6 G CARBOHYDRATE; 347 MG SODIUM; 43 MG CHOLESTEROL.

Cold Soba or Somen Noodles

½ lb. soba or somen noodles (*see* "The Well-Stocked Kitchen" *on page 221*)

2 tsp. sesame oil

2 tsp. reduced-sodium soy sauce

Bring a large pot of water to a boil. Slowly add noodles. When water returns to a boil, add ½ cup cold water. Repeat steps of returning water to a boil and adding cold water 2 or 3 times, until noodles are cooked through, about 3 minutes for somen or 4 minutes for soba noodles.

Drain the noodles in a colander and rinse well under cold water while working your fingers through the strands. Transfer to a serving bowl and toss with sesame oil and soy sauce.

Serves 4.

212 CALORIES PER SERVING: 8 G PROTEIN, 3 G FAT, 43 G CARBOHYDRATE; 550 MG SODIUM; 0 MG CHOLESTEROL.

Watercress Salad

2　Tbsp. reduced-sodium soy sauce
2　Tbsp. distilled white vinegar
1　Tbsp. sesame oil
2　bunches watercress, washed, dried and trimmed
　　freshly ground white or black pepper to taste

In a small salad bowl, whisk together soy sauce, vinegar and sesame oil. Add watercress and toss well. Season with pepper.

Serves 4.

37 CALORIES PER SERVING: 1 G PROTEIN, 3 G FAT, 1 G CARBOHYDRATE; 307 MG SODIUM; 0 MG CHOLESTEROL.

One from the Lime Latitudes

ime juice, bright and tart, is the flavor ribbon that winds through this menu from the tropics. Used almost as commonly as salt in many warm-weather cuisines, lime makes its first appearance here in the Yucatan-style chicken, where it is combined with orange and pineapple juice and herbs to form a spice baste. The flavorful chicken thighs are brushed with the piquant mixture as they roast. A bowlful of Caribbean rice and black beans and a stack of warm tortillas are the ubiquitous Latino accompaniment. Be sure to set a small plate of lime wedges on the table for squeezing over the rice or fresh beefsteak tomatoes. Lime juice takes its final bow at dessert, accenting sweet broiled pineapple.

Chicken Yucatan

3	Tbsp. orange juice
3	Tbsp. canned unsweetened pineapple juice
2	Tbsp. lime juice
2	Tbsp. chopped fresh oregano or 2 tsp. dried
1	Tbsp. olive oil
1	tsp. ground cumin
1	tsp. chili powder
1	clove garlic, finely chopped
½	tsp. salt
4-6	dashes Tabasco sauce
6	bone-in chicken thighs (2½ lbs.), skin and fat removed
	freshly ground black pepper to taste

Preheat oven to 375 degrees F. In a food processor or blender, combine

MENU

· ·

Chicken Yucatan

Caribbean Rice & Beans

(Sliced Tomatoes)

(Warm Corn Tortillas)

Broiled Pineapple

THIS MENU CONTAINS
785 CALORIES
PER SERVING WITH
21% OF CALORIES
FROM FAT.

Timetable

....

1. *Preheat oven to 375 degrees F.*

2. *Prepare and begin baking chicken.*

3. *Cut pineapple.*

4. *Make rice and beans.*

5. *Warm tortillas.*

6. *Preheat broiler for pineapple.*

orange, pineapple and lime juices, oregano, olive oil, cumin, chili powder, garlic, salt and Tabasco sauce; puree until smooth.

Set chicken thighs in an 8-by-11½-inch baking dish and brush with half of the citrus-herb mixture. Roast the chicken, turning once and brushing with the remaining citrus-herb mixture from time to time, for 30 to 35 minutes, or until the chicken is no longer pink in the center. Season with salt and pepper. Serve hot or cold.

Serves 6.

227 CALORIES PER SERVING: 25 G PROTEIN, 12 G FAT, 3 G CARBOHYDRATE; 257 MG SODIUM; 88 MG CHOLESTEROL.

Caribbean Rice & Beans

2	cups defatted reduced-sodium chicken stock
1	cup long-grain white rice
1½	tsp. olive oil
1	7½-oz. jar roasted red peppers (*see "The Well-Stocked Kitchen" on page 221*), drained and cut in short, thin strips
½	green bell pepper, cut in short, thin strips
2	cloves garlic, finely chopped
2	16-oz. cans black beans, drained and rinsed
2	Tbsp. distilled white vinegar
5-10	dashes Tabasco sauce
3	Tbsp. finely chopped fresh cilantro or oregano
	salt & freshly ground black pepper to taste

Combine chicken stock and rice in a medium-sized heavy saucepan; bring to a boil. Reduce heat to low, cover and simmer until the rice is tender and the liquid has been absorbed, 17 to 20 minutes. (*Alternatively, combine chicken stock and rice in a 2½-qt. casserole. Cover with lid and microwave on high power for 5 to 7 minutes, or until small bubbles appear around the edge. Stir once, cover dish and microwave on medium power—50 percent—for 17 to 20 minutes, or until tender. Let rice stand, covered, for 5 minutes.*)

Meanwhile, in a large nonstick skillet, heat oil over medium-high heat until hot but not smoking. Add red peppers, green peppers and garlic and sauté for 2 minutes. Add black beans, vinegar and Tabasco sauce. Bring the mixture to a boil, then reduce heat to low, cover and simmer for 5 minutes.

Stir in the reserved rice and cilantro or oregano. Taste and adjust seasonings. Serve with additional Tabasco sauce.

Serves 6.

311 CALORIES PER SERVING: 14 G PROTEIN, 2 G FAT, 59 G CARBOHYDRATE; 5 MG SODIUM; 0 MG CHOLESTEROL.

Broiled Pineapple

1 large pineapple, leaves, skin and eyes removed
2 tsp. vegetable oil, preferably canola oil
   freshly ground black pepper to taste
2 Tbsp. brown sugar
2 limes, quartered

Preheat broiler. With a sharp knife, cut pineapple crosswise into 8 slices, each about 1 inch thick. Brush the slices lightly with 1 tsp. of the oil, sprinkle with pepper and place in a single layer on a baking sheet.

Broil until lightly browned, about 7 minutes; flip the slices over, brush with remaining 1 tsp. oil, sprinkle with pepper and broil for 5 to 7 minutes longer.

Immediately sprinkle with brown sugar. Cut into wedges and serve with lime quarters for squeezing.

Serves 6.

113 CALORIES PER SERVING: 1 G PROTEIN, 2 G FAT, 26 G CARBOHYDRATE; 3 MG SODIUM; 0 MG CHOLESTEROL.

Grillwork

MENU

....

Swordfish Kebabs

Bruschetta with Tomatoes

Grilled Red Onions

Black Fruit Compote

THIS MENU CONTAINS
524 CALORIES
PER SERVING WITH
29% OF CALORIES
FROM FAT.

The pungent pine flavor of rosemary goes well with meaty swordfish, especially on the barbecue. (If you cannot find swordfish, fresh tuna, sea scallops or shrimp can be substituted.) For this recipe, chunks of the fish are briefly marinated, then threaded on skewers with fresh zucchini and grilled. The grill is also used for the *bruschetta*, which means "brushed" in Italian. The crisp Mediterranean toasts are a leaner alternative to American garlic bread and a perfect showcase for great home-grown tomatoes. Eating them is fun—and slightly messy. The grill also glamorizes red onions, which are tossed with a little olive oil. The dessert is a beautiful compote of dark-colored summer fruits—fresh blackberries, blueberries and cherries—in sweet port and orange juice.

Swordfish Kebabs

2 Tbsp. lemon juice

1 Tbsp. olive oil

1 Tbsp. chopped fresh rosemary or 1 tsp. dried

½ tsp. salt

¼ tsp. freshly ground black pepper

1 lb. swordfish steaks, cut into 1¼-inch cubes

1 small zucchini or summer squash, sliced into ¼-inch-thick ovals

Prepare a grill. If using wooden skewers, soak eight 10-inch skewers in water for 20 minutes.

In a shallow dish, stir together lemon juice, olive oil, rosemary, salt and pepper. Add swordfish and stir to coat well. Cover with plastic wrap and marinate in the refrigerator for 15 minutes.

Thread skewers alternately with pieces of swordfish and zucchini or summer squash. Grill the kebabs on a lightly oiled grill rack until the fish is opaque in the center, about 5 minutes per side.

Serves 4.

177 CALORIES PER SERVING: 23 G PROTEIN, 8 G FAT, 2 G CARBOHYDRATE; 370 MG SODIUM; 44 MG CHOLESTEROL.

Bruschetta with Tomatoes

2 large vine-ripened tomatoes, cored, seeded and chopped
2 Tbsp. chopped arugula (*see* "The Well-Stocked Kitchen" *on page 221*) or basil
2 tsp. olive oil, preferably extra-virgin
1 tsp. red-wine vinegar
½ tsp. finely chopped garlic
    salt & freshly ground black pepper to taste
8 ¾-inch-thick slices Italian bread

Prepare a grill. In a medium-sized bowl, stir together tomatoes, arugula or basil, olive oil, vinegar, garlic, salt and pepper. Set aside.

Grill bread on both sides until lightly toasted. Spoon the tomato mixture on top and serve immediately.

Serves 4.

168 CALORIES PER SERVING: 4 G PROTEIN, 5 G FAT, 25 G CARBOHYDRATE; 292 MG SODIUM; 0 MG CHOLESTEROL.

Timetable

....

1. *Preheat grill.*

2. *Cut up and marinate swordfish.*

3. *Make compote.*

4. *Slice bread and make tomato topping.*

5. *Prepare onions.*

6. *Slice zucchini; thread skewers.*

7. *Grill onions and bruschetta.*

8. *Grill kebabs.*

Grilled Red Onions

4 red onions
4 tsp. olive oil
  salt & freshly ground black pepper to taste

Prepare a grill. Peel onions and cut lengthwise into quarters, taking care to cut through the root to keep the quarters intact. In a small bowl, toss the onion quarters with oil to coat.

Grill, cut-side down, until well browned, about 5 minutes. Turn over and grill until browned and softened, about 5 minutes more. Transfer to a serving plate and season with salt and pepper.

Serves 4.

70 CALORIES PER SERVING: 1 G PROTEIN, 5 G FAT, 7 G CARBOHYDRATE; 2 MG SODIUM; 0 MG CHOLESTEROL.

Black Fruit Compote

2 Tbsp. honey
2 Tbsp. tawny port or Madeira
2 Tbsp. orange juice
1 cup blackberries
1 cup blueberries
1 cup pitted sweet cherries, cut in half
4 sprigs fresh mint (optional)

In a small saucepan, combine honey, port or Madeira and orange juice; stir over low heat just until blended. Let cool for 5 minutes.

Combine blackberries, blueberries and cherries in a medium-sized bowl and gently stir in the reserved honey mixture. Divide among 4 dessert dishes and garnish with fresh mint, if desired.

Serves 4.

127 CALORIES PER SERVING: 1 G PROTEIN, 1 G FAT, 29 G CARBOHYDRATE; 3 MG SODIUM; 0 MG CHOLESTEROL.

Rebirth of the Burger

This is an all-American backyard grill menu made healthier than the classic that inspired it. To cut down on the hamburger's fat, we mix in black beans. Sautéed onions, garlic and jalapeños contribute too. Although at their most flavorful on the grill, these burgers are also delicious broiled or cooked in a nonstick skillet. For texture, top them with shredded lettuce and your favorite salsa. The classic accompaniment is potato salad, crunchy with celery and flecked with herbs. Dessert is a deeply colored blueberry yogurt that's enlivened with fresh berries, lime juice and zest. It's a cool and refreshing meal-ender, one that could be made with raspberries or blackberries as well.

Chili Burgers

1	slice firm white bread, torn into small pieces
2	Tbsp. tomato paste
¾	lb. lean ground beef
⅔	cup canned black beans, drained, rinsed and coarsely chopped
2	Tbsp. chopped fresh cilantro or parsley
1	tsp. dried thyme leaves
½	tsp. salt
½	tsp. freshly ground black pepper
1	tsp. vegetable oil, preferably canola oil
1	small onion, finely chopped
1	clove garlic, finely chopped
1	jalapeño pepper, seeded and finely chopped
2	tsp. ground cumin

MENU

Chili Burgers

Herbed Potato Salad

Blueberry-Lime Yogurt

THIS MENU CONTAINS 796 CALORIES PER SERVING WITH 22% OF CALORIES FROM FAT.

4 onion rolls, split and toasted
 shredded lettuce for garnish
 tomato salsa or corn salsa for garnish

Prepare a grill or preheat the broiler. In a medium-sized bowl, use a fork to mash bread, tomato paste and 2 Tbsp. water to a paste. Add beef, beans, cilantro or parsley, thyme, salt and pepper. Set aside.

In a small nonstick skillet, heat oil over medium heat. Add onions and sauté until light golden, about 3 minutes. Add garlic, jalapeños and cumin; sauté until fragrant, about 2 minutes more. (If the mixture becomes too dry, add 1 Tbsp. water.) Let cool. Add to the reserved beef mixture and mix thoroughly but lightly. Shape into four ¾-inch patties.

Grill or broil the patties on a lightly oiled rack until browned and cooked through, about 5 minutes per side. Serve on rolls garnished with lettuce and tomato or corn salsa.

Serves 4.

433 CALORIES PER SERVING: 28 G PROTEIN, 15 G FAT, 48 G CARBOHYDRATE; 677 MG SODIUM; 65 MG CHOLESTEROL.

Herbed Potato Salad

1½ lbs. red or Yukon Gold potatoes, scrubbed and cut into
 1-inch pieces.
 1 tsp. salt, plus more to taste
1½ tsp. sherry vinegar or white-wine vinegar
 freshly ground black pepper to taste
 ¼ cup nonfat plain yogurt
 2 Tbsp. reduced-fat mayonnaise
 1 Tbsp. Dijon mustard
 ⅓ cup chopped celery
 ¼ cup chopped scallions
 1 Tbsp. chopped fresh parsley
 1 Tbsp. chopped fresh dill (optional)

Timetable

1. Drain yogurt for dessert.

2. Cook blueberries.

3. Make potato salad.

4. Preheat grill or broiler.

5. Prepare and grill chili burgers.

In a medium-sized saucepan, cover potatoes with cold water and add 1 tsp. salt. Bring to a boil and cook over medium heat until tender, 7 to 9 minutes. Drain in a colander and transfer to a large bowl. Toss with vinegar and season generously with pepper. Set the potatoes aside to cool.

In a small bowl, whisk together yogurt, mayonnaise and mustard. Add the dressing to the reserved potatoes along with celery, scallions, parsley and dill, if using, stirring gently to combine. Season with salt and pepper.

Serves 4.

178 CALORIES PER SERVING: 4 G PROTEIN, 2 G FAT, 36 G CARBOHYDRATE; 571 MG SODIUM; 3 MG CHOLESTEROL.

Blueberry-Lime Yogurt

     3   cups low-fat vanilla yogurt
     2   cups fresh blueberries
     3   Tbsp. lime juice
     2   Tbsp. sugar
    1½   tsp. grated lime zest, plus 4 strips lime zest for garnish

Line a large sieve with cheesecloth or coffee filters and set it over a bowl; spoon in yogurt. Place in the refrigerator to drain for about 30 minutes.

Meanwhile, combine blueberries, lime juice, sugar and lime zest in a medium-sized saucepan. Stir over medium heat until the berries are just beginning to break down and release their juices, 2 to 3 minutes. Transfer to a bowl and refrigerate.

Just before serving, add the drained yogurt to the cooled berries and stir to combine. Garnish with strips of lime zest.

Serves 4.

247 CALORIES PER SERVING: 10 G PROTEIN, 3 G FAT, 47 G CARBOHYDRATE; 124 MG SODIUM; 10 MG CHOLESTEROL.

An Hour in Provence

In Provence, *pan bagna* means moist bread, but the name certainly doesn't say it all. This is a hearty, stuffed-loaf sandwich, where the bread is scooped out and incorporated with the filling to absorb the garlicky juice. We've added tuna to the classic tomato-based filling; the Italian olive oil-packed variety of tuna is tastier, but rinse it first. Use a good, crusty French bread and fresh thyme, if possible. The salad offers more hearty Mediterranean flavors; pureed garlic and anchovies add depth to the dressing and rings of red onion add bite before it is topped off with Parmesan cheese. Pairing basil with fresh peaches for dessert works surprisingly well. The sliced peaches are poached, then enriched with a little butter, vanilla and the fresh, fragrant basil leaves.

MENU

....

Pan Bagna

Romaine Salad with Garlic Dressing

Peach Compote with Basil

Pan Bagna

1	16-inch-long loaf of French bread
¼	cup lemon juice
1	Tbsp. olive oil, preferably extra-virgin
1	clove garlic, finely chopped
1	6⅛-oz. can tuna, packed in olive oil, drained, rinsed and squeezed dry, or packed in water, squeezed dry
1	large vine-ripened tomato, cored, seeded and chopped
1	red bell pepper, cored, seeded and chopped
2	scallions, trimmed and chopped
2	Tbsp. chopped pitted black olives, preferably Kalamata
1½	Tbsp. capers, rinsed
1	tsp. chopped fresh thyme or ¼ tsp. dried thyme leaves
	salt & freshly ground black pepper to taste

THIS MENU CONTAINS 792 CALORIES PER SERVING WITH 20% OF CALORIES FROM FAT.

Timetable

....

1. *Simmer garlic for salad dressing.*

2. *Make peach compote.*

3. *Wash romaine; finish salad dressing.*

4. *Make pan bagna.*

Cut bread in half lengthwise. Scoop out crumbs from both halves, leaving ½-inch-thick shells.

In a food processor or blender, process the crumbs until finely chopped; set aside.

In a large bowl, whisk together lemon juice, oil and garlic. Stir in the reserved breadcrumbs, tuna, tomatoes, bell peppers, scallions, olives, capers and thyme; mix well. Season with salt and pepper. Spoon the breadcrumb mixture into the bottom bread shell and replace the top. Cut crosswise to serve.

Serves 4.

452 CALORIES PER SERVING: 23 G PROTEIN, 7 G FAT, 69 G CARBOHYDRATE; 849 MG SODIUM; 13 MG CHOLESTEROL.

Romaine Salad with Garlic Dressing

....

GARLIC DRESSING

- 2 small heads garlic, separated into cloves
- ½ cup defatted reduced-sodium chicken or vegetable stock
- 3 Tbsp. white-wine or cider vinegar
- 1½ Tbsp. olive oil, preferably extra-virgin
- 1½ tsp. Dijon mustard
- 2 anchovy fillets, rinsed and patted dry
  salt & freshly ground black pepper to taste

ROMAINE SALAD

- 8 cups washed, dried and torn romaine lettuce
- 1 small red onion, peeled, sliced and separated into rings
- 6 anchovy fillets, rinsed, patted dry and cut in half lengthwise
- 2 Tbsp. freshly grated Parmesan cheese
  freshly ground black pepper to taste

To make dressing: In a small saucepan, bring unpeeled garlic cloves and stock to a simmer over medium-low heat. Reduce heat to very low, cover and cook until the cloves are tender, about 15 minutes. Remove the cloves with a slotted spoon to a plate to cool for 2 minutes, reserving the cooking liquid. Add enough water to the cooking liquid to measure ¼ cup.

Squeeze cooled garlic pulp out of the skins into a blender or food processor. Add reserved cooking liquid, vinegar, oil, mustard and the 2 anchovies; process or blend until smooth. Season with salt and pepper.

To make salad: In a large bowl, combine lettuce, onion rings and garlic dressing. Toss well and top with the 6 halved anchovies, Parmesan cheese and freshly ground black pepper.

Serves 4.

113 CALORIES PER SERVING: 6 G PROTEIN, 7 G FAT, 8 G CARBOHYDRATE; 367 MG SODIUM; 10 MG CHOLESTEROL.

Peach Compote with Basil

½ cup sugar
2 lbs. peaches (5-6), peeled, pitted and sliced
4 tsp. butter, cut into small pieces
½ cup loosely packed fresh basil leaves
½ tsp. pure vanilla extract

In a medium-sized skillet, combine sugar and 1 cup water; cook, stirring, over medium heat until the sugar dissolves, 1 to 2 minutes. Add peaches and simmer for 2 minutes. Add butter, stirring until melted. Add basil leaves and cook just until wilted, about 30 seconds. Stir in vanilla and serve warm or at room temperature.

Serves 4.

227 CALORIES PER SERVING: 2 G PROTEIN, 4 G FAT, 50 G CARBOHYDRATE; 40 MG SODIUM; 10 MG CHOLESTEROL.

Our Idea of Finger Food

MENU

....

Zucchini &
Carrot Sticks with
Black-Eyed
Pea Dip

Grilled Orange
Chicken Fingers

Penne & Roasted
Pepper Salad

Summer
Blackberries

THIS MENU CONTAINS
764 CALORIES
PER SERVING WITH
19% OF CALORIES
FROM FAT.

Kids should enjoy this menu, because they can eat both the chicken and the veggies with their fingers. The simple, sweet glaze can be whipped up fast; marinating time is just 15 minutes and the marinade caramelizes deliciously on the grill. A puree of black-eyed peas freshened with lemon juice, parsley, tarragon and garlic makes a great dip for fresh zucchini and carrot slices. Pasta salad has become a summer dinner classic; this one includes convenient roasted red peppers and capers for extra zip. Depending on the audience, you might want to make the dressing livelier with more cayenne or balsamic vinegar. Summer Blackberries is an old-fashioned way to dress up a glorious summer berry.

Zucchini & Carrot Sticks with Black-Eyed Pea Dip

1	15½-oz. can black-eyed peas, drained and rinsed
¼	cup packed fresh parsley leaves
2	Tbsp. lemon juice
2	Tbsp. olive oil, preferably extra-virgin
1½	tsp. chopped garlic
1½	tsp. chopped fresh tarragon or ½ tsp. dried
¼	tsp. freshly ground black pepper
	salt to taste
4	small carrots, peeled and cut into sticks
1	medium zucchini, cut into ¼-inch-thick slices

Place peas, parsley, lemon juice, olive oil, garlic, tarragon and pepper in a food processor. Process until smooth. Taste and adjust seasonings, adding salt if desired.

Transfer to a serving bowl and serve with fresh carrots and zucchini for dipping.

Makes about 1¼ cups.

Serves 4.

190 CALORIES PER SERVING: 5 G PROTEIN, 7 G FAT, 28 G CARBOHYDRATE; 30 MG SODIUM; 0 MG CHOLESTEROL.

Grilled Orange Chicken Fingers

1	lb. boneless, skinless chicken breasts, fat trimmed
1½	Tbsp. Dijon mustard
1½	Tbsp. frozen orange-juice concentrate, thawed
1½	Tbsp. honey
1	tsp. sesame oil
½	tsp. freshly ground black pepper
	salt to taste

Cut chicken crosswise into ¾-inch-wide strips. In a medium-sized bowl, whisk together mustard, orange-juice concentrate, honey, sesame oil and pepper until smooth. Add the chicken strips and toss to combine. Cover and marinate in the refrigerator for about 15 minutes.

Meanwhile, prepare grill or preheat the broiler. Lightly oil rack or coat it with nonstick cooking spray. Remove the chicken strips from the marinade, discarding any extra marinade. Grill or broil for 2 to 3 minutes per side, or until no longer pink in the center. Season with salt and serve.

Serves 4.

168 CALORIES PER SERVING: 26 G PROTEIN, 3 G FAT, 9 G CARBOHYDRATE; 79 MG SODIUM; 66 MG CHOLESTEROL.

Timetable

1. *Heat water for pasta.*

2. *Marinate chicken.*

3. *Preheat grill or broiler.*

4. *Cook pasta; make salad.*

5. *Make pea spread; cut vegetables.*

6. *Make dessert.*

7. *Cook chicken.*

Penne & Roasted Pepper Salad

10 oz. penne (*see* "The Well-Stocked Kitchen" *on page 221*) or rotini

1 7½-oz. jar roasted red peppers (*see* "The Well-Stocked Kitchen" *on page 221*), drained and diced

¼ cup chopped fresh basil or parsley, plus leaves for garnish

3 Tbsp. capers, rinsed

2 scallions, trimmed and finely chopped

1 clove garlic, finely chopped

2 Tbsp. balsamic vinegar, or more to taste

1½ Tbsp. olive oil, preferably extra-virgin

salt & freshly ground black pepper to taste

pinch cayenne pepper

In a large pot of boiling salted water, cook penne or rotini until al dente, 6 to 8 minutes. Drain in a colander and rinse well with cold water.

Transfer to a large bowl; add roasted peppers, chopped basil or parsley, capers, scallions, garlic, vinegar and oil. Season with salt, pepper and cayenne. Garnish with basil or parsley leaves.

Serves 4.

330 CALORIES PER SERVING: 10 G PROTEIN, 6 G FAT, 58 G CARBOHYDRATE; 145 MG SODIUM; 0 MG CHOLESTEROL.

Summer Blackberries

3 Tbsp. orange juice

1 Tbsp. lemon juice

1 Tbsp. sugar

1 tsp. grated lemon zest

3 cups fresh blackberries

In a medium-sized serving bowl, combine orange juice, lemon juice, sugar and zest, stirring to dissolve sugar. Add blackberries and toss to combine.

Serves 4.

76 CALORIES PER SERVING: 1 G PROTEIN, 0 G FAT, 19 G CARBOHYDRATE; 1 MG SODIUM; 0 MG CHOLESTEROL.

One Arabian Night

THIS MENU CONTAINS
738 CALORIES
PER SERVING WITH
23% OF CALORIES
FROM FAT.

Middle Eastern flavors have inspired this light vegetarian menu for a warm summer evening. For the main course, slices of eggplant are quickly roasted in the oven, then wrapped around a filling of whole-wheat couscous accented with fresh mint and feta cheese; your favorite spaghetti sauce is spooned over the top. A salad of grated carrots flavored with garlic and cumin and flecked with a handful of parsley is a colorful accompaniment. Warmed pita bread rounds out the meal. It somehow seems appropriate that the dinner end with peaches. Ripe, juicy peaches are one of summer's real treats. They were once thought to have originated in ancient Persia, hence their family name *Prunus persica*. Here, baked in a lemon-ginger syrup, they are divine.

Eggplant-Couscous Rolls

2   1-lb. eggplants
4   tsp. olive oil
1   cup couscous, preferably whole-wheat
½   tsp. dried thyme leaves
½   tsp. salt
¾   cup plus 2 Tbsp. crumbled feta cheese
3   Tbsp. chopped fresh mint
    freshly ground black pepper to taste
1   cup spaghetti sauce

Preheat oven to 425 degrees F. Lightly oil two baking sheets or coat them with nonstick cooking spray. Trim both ends of the eggplants. Stand one eggplant on end and remove a thin slice of skin from two opposite sides and discard. Repeat with the second eggplant. Cut each

Timetable

....

1. *Preheat oven to 425 degrees F.*

2. *Roast eggplants.*

3. *Make couscous and let cool.*

4. *Prepare and bake peaches.*

5. *Finish and bake eggplant rolls.*

6. *Make carrot salad.*

7. *Warm pita bread.*

eggplant lengthwise into 6 or more ⅜-inch-thick slices. Using 2 tsp. of the oil, brush both sides of the slices and arrange in a single layer on the baking sheets.

Bake for 10 minutes, turn over and bake for about 10 to 15 minutes more, or until lightly browned and tender.

Meanwhile, in a medium-sized saucepan, bring 1½ cups water to a boil. Stir in couscous, thyme, salt and remaining 2 tsp. olive oil. Remove from the heat, cover and let stand for 5 minutes, or until the water is absorbed. Uncover and let cool for 15 minutes. With a fork, stir in ¾ cup of the feta, 2 Tbsp. of the mint and pepper.

Lightly oil a 9-by-13-inch baking dish or coat it with nonstick cooking spray. Place some of the couscous mixture in the center of each eggplant slice. Roll up the eggplant firmly around the filling and place, seam-side down, in the prepared dish. Cover with foil and bake for 15 minutes. Uncover, spoon spaghetti sauce on top and bake for 5 minutes more. Sprinkle with the remaining 2 Tbsp. feta cheese and 1 Tbsp. mint.

Serves 4.

401 CALORIES PER SERVING: 14 G PROTEIN, 12 G FAT, 65 G CARBOHYDRATE; 899 MG SODIUM; 22 MG CHOLESTEROL.

Carrot Salad with Cumin

6 carrots (about 1 lb.) peeled and coarsely grated
½ cup chopped fresh parsley, preferably Italian
1 Tbsp. lemon juice
1 Tbsp. olive oil, preferably extra-virgin
1 clove garlic, finely chopped
½ tsp. ground cumin
 salt & freshly ground black pepper to taste

In a medium-sized bowl, toss all ingredients. Serve within 1 hour.

Serves 4.

85 CALORIES PER SERVING: 1 G PROTEIN, 4 G FAT, 13 G CARBOHYDRATE; 43 MG SODIUM; 0 MG CHOLESTEROL.

Gingered Peach Gratin

⅓ cup sugar

¼ cup lemon juice

½ tsp. ground ginger

4 peaches (1¼ lbs.), cut in half and pitted

4 gingersnaps, crushed

Preheat oven to 425 degrees F. In a small saucepan, combine sugar, lemon juice, ginger and 2 Tbsp. water; bring to a simmer.

Place the peaches, cut-side up, in a shallow 1-qt. baking dish. Pour the ginger syrup over the peaches and sprinkle with gingersnap crumbs. Bake for 15 to 20 minutes, or until the peaches are tender when pierced with a knife and the syrup has thickened. Serve warm or at room temperature, with the sauce spooned over.

Serves 4.

147 CALORIES PER SERVING: 2 G PROTEIN, 2 G FAT, 35 G CARBOHYDRATE; 20 MG SODIUM; 0 MG CHOLESTEROL.

The Magic of Fish & Ginger

MENU

....

*Salmon in a
Vibrant Sauce*

*Swiss Chard
& Sweet Pepper
Stir-Fry*

(Basmati Rice)

*Strawberries with
Minted Yogurt*

THIS MENU CONTAINS
556 CALORIES
PER SERVING WITH
19% OF CALORIES
FROM FAT.

O n busy days, fish is a first choice for a quick, elegant dinner. Fillets will cook in minutes, readily taking on the seasonings of spicy marinades. For this menu, pieces of salmon or halibut marinate for five to 10 minutes in a blend of fresh cilantro, ginger, garlic, lime juice, jalapeños and turmeric; the marinade becomes the sauce when the fish is steamed for a few minutes in a covered skillet. Swiss Chard & Sweet Pepper Stir-Fry is a colorful and full-flavored pairing for the fish. The perfume of cooking basmati rice will fill the kitchen as you chop and slice ingredients for the main course and vegetable side dish. For dessert, yogurt, buttermilk and fresh mint make a simple sauce to serve over strawberries.

Salmon in a Vibrant Sauce

¼   cup chopped fresh cilantro
3   Tbsp. chopped fresh ginger
2   Tbsp. coarsely chopped garlic
2   jalapeño peppers, seeded and coarsely chopped
3   Tbsp. lime juice
1   Tbsp. vegetable oil, preferably canola oil
½   tsp. salt
¼   tsp. turmeric
1¼ lbs. salmon or halibut fillet, cut into 2-by-2-inch pieces

Using a food processor or a mortar and pestle, grind together cilantro, ginger, garlic and jalapeños until blended into a smooth paste, adding a little water if necessary. Add lime juice, oil, salt and turmeric and mix well.

Transfer to a shallow glass or ceramic dish, add the fish pieces and toss in this marinade, making sure each piece is well coated. Cover and refrigerate for 5 to 10 minutes.

Coat the bottom of a large nonstick skillet with 3 to 4 Tbsp. of the marinade. Transfer the fish to the skillet and cover with the remaining marinade. Cover the skillet with a tight-fitting lid and place over medium-low heat. Cook gently until the interior of the fish is opaque, 5 to 10 minutes. (Cooking time will vary with the thickness of the fillet.)

(Alternatively, cover the dish used for marinating with vented plastic wrap and microwave on high power for 5 to 8 minutes, rotating once, or just until the interior of the fish is opaque.)

Serves 4.

201 CALORIES PER SERVING: 30 G PROTEIN, 7 G FAT, 4 G CARBOHYDRATE; 347 MG SODIUM; 45 MG CHOLESTEROL.

Swiss Chard & Sweet Pepper Stir-Fry

1 Tbsp. vegetable oil, preferably canola oil
1 onion, cut in half and thinly sliced
1 large red bell pepper, cored, seeded and thinly sliced
3 Tbsp. vegetable stock or water
1½ tsp. hoisin sauce
1 lb. Swiss chard, washed, stems diced, leaves shredded (6 cups)
   salt to taste

Heat oil in a wok or large deep skillet over high heat. Add onions and stir-fry until they are translucent and slightly soft, about 2 minutes. Add peppers, stock or water and hoisin sauce; bring to a boil. Reduce heat to medium-low and simmer, covered, for 2 to 3 minutes. Add chard stems and leaves, tossing to combine. Simmer, covered, just until the chard is tender, 3 to 5 minutes. Season with salt.

Serves 4.

75 CALORIES PER SERVING: 3 G PROTEIN, 4 G FAT, 10 G CARBOHYDRATE; 304 MG SODIUM; 0 MG CHOLESTEROL.

Timetable

1. *Make minted yogurt.*

2. *Slice strawberries.*

3. *Make marinade; add fish.*

4. *Cook rice.*

5. *Prepare stir-fry ingredients.*

6. *Cook fish.*

7. *Stir-fry vegetables.*

Strawberries with Minted Yogurt

½ cup nonfat plain yogurt

½ cup buttermilk

1 Tbsp. sugar or to taste

½ Tbsp. chopped fresh mint

⅛ tsp. pure vanilla extract

1 pt. strawberries, hulled and sliced

In a small bowl, whisk together yogurt, buttermilk, sugar, chopped mint and vanilla until smooth.

Spoon strawberries into individual dishes and drizzle with the yogurt sauce.

Serves 4.

57 CALORIES PER SERVING: 3 G PROTEIN, 1 G FAT, 10 G CARBOHYDRATE; 55 MG SODIUM; 2 MG CHOLESTEROL.

Chicken Wearing a Bow Tie

On a hot summer's eve, this is a great light supper. The chicken and pasta salad is virtually a one-dish meal. It includes tender poached breasts, bow-tie pasta, fresh red bell peppers, celery and scallions, all tossed with a lively dressing. Next, served at room temperature, bright green snow peas, flavored with garlic and fresh orange, make a pretty accompaniment. Dessert is also delightful in its simplicity. Ripe nectarines are halved, pitted, then baked with a little sugar to soften them. They make their own rosy syrup, perfumed with vanilla, which is brushed over them.

MENU

....

*Chicken &
Bow Ties Salad*

*Snow Peas
with Orange*

Vanilla Nectarines

Chicken & Bow Ties Salad

- 1 lb. boneless, skinless chicken breasts, fat trimmed
- ½ lb. bow-tie pasta
- 1 Tbsp. sesame seeds
- ¼ cup rice-wine vinegar
- 2 Tbsp. Dijon mustard
- 1 Tbsp. finely chopped fresh ginger
- 1 Tbsp. sesame oil
- 1½ tsp. reduced-sodium soy sauce
- 1½ tsp. sugar
- 1 red bell pepper, cored, seeded, quartered and thinly sliced
- 2 stalks celery, sliced
- 4 scallions, thinly sliced
  salt & freshly ground black pepper to taste

Cover chicken breasts with plastic wrap and flatten them slightly with a heavy skillet or rolling pin. Remove the wrap, arrange the breasts in a single layer in a deep skillet or wide saucepan and cover with cold water.

THIS MENU CONTAINS
631 CALORIES
PER SERVING WITH
13% OF CALORIES
FROM FAT.

Timetable
·····························

1. *Preheat oven to 425 degrees F.*

2. *Heat water for pasta.*

3. *Poach chicken.*

4. *Bake nectarines.*

5. *Cook pasta; finish salad.*

6. *Make snow peas.*

Slowly bring to a simmer over low heat. Once simmering, turn the breasts over, cover and remove from the heat. Let sit for 15 to 20 minutes, or until no longer pink in the center. Transfer the cooked breasts to a cutting board and let cool slightly.

Meanwhile, cook pasta in a large pot of boiling salted water until al dente, about 10 minutes. Drain the pasta and rinse under cold water until cool. Drain well.

While the pasta cooks, stir sesame seeds in a small dry skillet over medium heat until toasted, about 1 minute; transfer to a large bowl. Whisk in vinegar, mustard, ginger, sesame oil, soy sauce and sugar. Thinly slice the chicken and add to the bowl, along with the pasta, red peppers, celery and scallions. Toss and season with salt and pepper.

Serves 4.

479 CALORIES PER SERVING: 37 G PROTEIN, 7 G FAT, 64 G CARBOHYDRATE; 192 MG SODIUM; 66 MG CHOLESTEROL.

Snow Peas with Orange
·····························

1	tsp. vegetable oil, preferably canola oil
1	tsp. finely chopped garlic
	grated zest of 1 orange
½	lb. snow peas, stems and strings removed (3 cups)
2	Tbsp. orange juice
	salt & freshly ground black pepper to taste

Heat oil in a medium-sized skillet over medium heat. Add garlic and orange zest, and cook, stirring, until golden, about 30 seconds. Add snow peas and orange juice.

Cover and cook until the peas are tender, 2 to 3 minutes. Uncover the pan and cook until the juices thicken slightly, about 1 minute. Season with salt and pepper.

Serves 4.

61 CALORIES PER SERVING: 3 G PROTEIN, 1 G FAT, 11 G CARBOHYDRATE; 5 MG SODIUM; 0 MG CHOLESTEROL.

Vanilla Nectarines

4 nectarines, cut in half and pitted

2 Tbsp. sugar

½ tsp. pure vanilla extract

Preheat oven to 425 degrees F. Place nectarines skin-side down in a small pie plate or small baking dish. Add ¼ cup water.

In a small bowl, stir together sugar and vanilla until completely combined. Spoon the vanilla-sugar mixture into the cavity of each nectarine.

Cover the pan tightly with foil and bake for 20 minutes. Uncover the pan and bake for about 15 minutes more, or until the nectarines are tender and the juices are syrupy. (Add more water if the juices begin to scorch.) Brush the nectarines with the syrup from the bottom of the dish. Serve warm or at room temperature.

Serves 4.

91 CALORIES PER SERVING: 1 G PROTEIN, 1 G FAT, 22 G CARBOHYDRATE; 0 MG SODIUM; 0 MG CHOLESTEROL.

Salad to Start, Soup to Finish

MENU
....

Grilled Sirloin Salad

Tomato-Garlic Toasts

Cold Plum Soup

THIS MENU CONTAINS
528 CALORIES
PER SERVING WITH
27% CALORIES
FROM FAT.

Here's a switch—a beef salad to start and a cool plum soup to end the meal. The beauty of this menu is that its preparation does not heat up the kitchen; the beef, vegetables and toasts are all cooked on an outdoor grill. Be sure to choose a lean grade of beef—Select, not Prime—for the sirloin, and be careful not to overcook it. The plums for the soup simmer for 10 minutes on the stovetop, just long enough to make them tender and sweet. Then they are pureed with ice cubes; this helps to cool down the soup quickly.

Grilled Sirloin Salad

2 Tbsp. reduced-sodium soy sauce
2 Tbsp. balsamic vinegar
2 tsp. sesame oil
2 tsp. brown sugar
1 tsp. finely chopped fresh ginger
1 clove garlic, finely chopped
2 tsp. black peppercorns, crushed
¾ lb. beef sirloin, trimmed of visible fat
   salt to taste
16 scallions, white part only
1 red bell pepper, cored, seeded and cut in half lengthwise
12 cups washed, dried and torn salad greens, such as escarole, curly endive, radicchio or watercress

Prepare a grill. In a blender or food processor, combine soy sauce, vinegar, oil, sugar, ginger and garlic; blend until smooth and set aside.
  Press peppercorns into both sides of the meat. Season lightly with salt.

Place the meat, scallions and red pepper halves on the grill and cook for 4 minutes. Turn the meat and vegetables and cook until the meat is medium-rare and the vegetables are slightly charred, 3 to 4 minutes more.

Let the meat stand for 5 minutes before cutting it, against the grain, into very thin slices. Cut the scallions into 1-inch pieces. Slice the peppers into long strips.

Toss greens with the reserved dressing. Place on a serving platter or 4 plates. Arrange the meat and grilled vegetables over the top and serve.

Serves 4.

218 CALORIES PER SERVING: 23 G PROTEIN, 9 G FAT, 12 G CARBOHYDRATE; 397 MG SODIUM; 57 MG CHOLESTEROL.

Tomato-Garlic Toasts

½   1-lb. loaf Italian or French bread
2   Tbsp. chopped fresh parsley, preferably Italian
1   Tbsp. olive oil, preferably extra-virgin
1   Tbsp. nonfat plain yogurt
1   Tbsp. tomato paste
1   clove garlic, finely chopped
    salt & freshly ground black pepper to taste

Prepare a grill. Cut bread in half lengthwise, then cut each piece in half.

In a small bowl, combine parsley, oil, yogurt, tomato paste, garlic, salt and pepper. Toast the bread on the grill, cut-side down. Spread with the tomato-garlic mixture and serve warm.

Serves 4.

179 CALORIES PER SERVING: 6 G PROTEIN, 4 G FAT, 30 G CARBOHYDRATE; 349 MG SODIUM; 0 MG CHOLESTEROL.

Timetable

1. Preheat grill.

2. Make plum soup.

3. Make salad dressing.

4. Make tomato-garlic spread.

5. Wash greens.

6. Grill beef, vegetables and bread.

Cold Plum Soup

½ cup frozen apple-juice concentrate
1 lb. plums (about 5), pitted and coarsely chopped
1 cinnamon stick
1½ cups nonfat plain yogurt

In a large heavy saucepan, bring apple-juice concentrate to a boil. Reduce heat to low, add plums and cinnamon stick, cover, and simmer until the plums are tender, about 10 minutes. Discard the cinnamon stick.

Transfer the mixture to a blender, add 3 ice cubes and puree until smooth. Pour into a bowl and whisk in yogurt. Cover and refrigerate until chilled, about 45 minutes.

Serves 4.

113 CALORIES PER SERVING: 6 G PROTEIN, 1 G FAT, 22 G CARBOHYDRATE; 66 MG SODIUM; 2 MG CHOLESTEROL.

Presto! Penne & Peas

MENU
....

*Penne with
Sugar Snap Peas*

Marinated Carrots

*Lemon
Frozen Yogurt
with Berries*

THIS MENU CONTAINS
601 CALORIES
PER SERVING WITH
13% OF CALORIES
FROM FAT.

Cherry tomatoes, little gems of flavor, are plentiful throughout the summer. This pasta dish makes use of them in combination with sweet sugar snap peas. Toasted pine nuts add crunch and golden color to this light, summery pasta dish. The carrots are slightly pickled, a refreshingly tart and crunchy companion to the pasta. Cut into julienne sticks and just barely cooked, they're tossed with the dressing while still hot, permitting them to absorb its flavor as they cool. Dessert is nonfat frozen yogurt dressed up with lemon juice and zest and smothered in juicy fresh berries.

Penne with Sugar Snap Peas

¼ cup pine nuts

1 pt. cherry tomatoes, quartered

6 Tbsp. snipped fresh chives

2 Tbsp. olive oil, preferably extra-virgin

½ tsp. sugar

½ tsp. salt, plus more to taste

1 lb. sugar snap peas, strings removed, pods cut in half diagonally

1 lb. penne (*see* "The Well-Stocked Kitchen" *on page 221*)

½ cup slivered fresh basil

½ cup chopped fresh parsley
   freshly ground black pepper to taste

In a small dry skillet over medium heat, toast pine nuts, stirring, until fragrant and lightly browned, 3 to 4 minutes. Coarsely chop the nuts and set aside.

Bring a large pot of salted water to a boil. In a large serving bowl, combine tomatoes, 4 Tbsp. of the chives, olive oil, sugar and ½ tsp. salt.

Place snap peas in a sieve, then dip into the boiling water for about 1½ minutes, or until not quite cooked through. Lift out and set aside. Add penne to the water; boil until al dente, 6 to 8 minutes. Drain and add to the serving bowl containing the tomatoes. Add the reserved snap peas, basil, parsley and remaining 2 Tbsp. chives and toss. Season with salt and pepper. Sprinkle with the reserved pine nuts, toss again and serve.

Serves 4.

310 CALORIES PER SERVING: 11 G PROTEIN, 7 G FAT, 52 G CARBOHYDRATE; 148 MG SODIUM; 0 MG CHOLESTEROL.

Marinated Carrots

6   carrots (¾ lb.), cut into ¼-inch-by-2-inch julienne
4   cloves garlic, peeled and crushed
1   Tbsp. balsamic vinegar
2   tsp. olive oil, preferably extra-virgin
2   tsp. chopped fresh thyme or ½ tsp. dried thyme leaves
    pinch sugar
    salt & freshly ground black pepper to taste

Place carrots and garlic in a small saucepan and cover with cold water. Bring to a boil over medium-high heat and boil for 30 seconds. (*Alternatively, place carrots, garlic and ¼ cup water in a 1-qt. casserole; cover with lid or vented plastic wrap and microwave on high power for 5 to 7 minutes, stirring midway, or until crisp-tender.*) Immediately drain the carrots and garlic; transfer to a medium-sized bowl. Add vinegar, oil, thyme and sugar and toss well. Let cool for 10 minutes, stirring occasionally. Discard the garlic cloves and season with salt and pepper.

Serves 4.

65 CALORIES PER SERVING: 1 G PROTEIN, 2 G FAT, 11 G CARBOHYDRATE; 31 MG SODIUM; 0 MG CHOLESTEROL.

Timetable

1. *Make lemon frozen yogurt.*

2. *Heat water for pasta.*

3. *Make marinated carrots.*

4. *Make pasta.*

5. *Toss berries with sugar.*

6. *Finish pasta dish.*

Lemon Frozen Yogurt with Berries

¼ cup plus 1 Tbsp. sugar, preferably superfine
¼ cup lemon juice
2 tsp. grated lemon zest
3 cups nonfat vanilla frozen yogurt
1 cup fresh raspberries or sliced fresh strawberries

In a small bowl, stir together ¼ cup of the sugar, lemon juice and lemon zest until the sugar is dissolved.

Soften frozen yogurt in the microwave at medium-low power (30 percent) for 30 to 60 seconds. (*Alternatively, allow the frozen yogurt to soften for 10 to 20 minutes at room temperature.*) Transfer to a bowl and with a wooden spoon or whisk, stir in the sugar-lemon juice mixture.

Scoop the mixture into dessert dishes, cover with plastic wrap and return to the freezer to firm up for about 30 minutes.

Meanwhile, in a small bowl stir together berries and remaining 1 Tbsp. sugar and let stand until the berries are juicy, about 15 minutes. Spoon over the top of the frozen yogurt.

Serves 4.

226 CALORIES PER SERVING: 3 G PROTEIN, 0 G FAT, 53 G CARBOHYDRATE; 53 MG SODIUM; 0 MG CHOLESTEROL.

Seoul Supper

Finger food is always fun, especially when it's colorful and unusual, as it is in this Korean menu. The pancakes combine shrimp and julienned vegetables in a light batter. Cut into wedges, the pancakes are dipped in a sweet-tart scallion and sesame sauce. Although sticky rice usually requires hours of pre-soaking, this method puts it within the grasp of a pressed-for-time cook. Every Korean dinner includes kimchee, a fiery pickled cabbage now available in the produce section of many supermarkets. Fresh fruit is a traditional and appropriate way to end a Korean meal. Here, strawberries are stirred together with a little sugar, orange juice and crystallized ginger, then sprinkled with toasted pine nuts.

Korean Shrimp Pancakes

DIPPING SAUCE

1	tsp. sesame seeds
3	Tbsp. reduced-sodium soy sauce
1	scallion, trimmed and finely chopped
1½	tsp. rice vinegar or cider vinegar
1	tsp. sugar

SCALLION PANCAKES

3	large eggs
4	large egg whites
1½	cups all-purpose white flour
1	Tbsp. plus 4 tsp. vegetable oil, preferably canola oil
¼	tsp. salt
¼	lb. small cooked shrimp

MENU

....

Korean Shrimp Pancakes

Sticky Rice with Peas

(Kimchee)

Strawberries with Ginger & Pine Nuts

THIS MENU CONTAINS 620 CALORIES PER SERVING WITH 20% OF CALORIES FROM FAT.

Timetable

....

1. *Cook rice.*

2. *Make pancake dipping sauce and batter; prepare filling.*

3. *Prepare dessert.*

4. *Cook pancakes.*

10 scallions, trimmed, quartered lengthwise and cut into 3-inch lengths

1 small zucchini, trimmed and sliced into fine julienne (3 inches long)

1 large carrot, peeled and sliced into fine julienne (3 inches long)

¼ cup chopped fresh chives

To make dipping sauce: In a small dry skillet over medium-high heat, stir sesame seeds until lightly toasted, 2 to 3 minutes. Transfer to a small bowl and add soy sauce, scallions, vinegar and sugar.

To make pancake batter: In a medium-sized bowl, beat 1 egg and 2 eggs whites together with a fork. Whisk in flour, 1 Tbsp. of the oil, salt and 1 cup water; the batter should be smooth and medium thick. Let rest for 15 to 20 minutes.

To cook pancakes: In a small bowl, lightly beat the remaining 2 eggs plus 2 egg whites. Heat a small nonstick skillet over medium-low heat. Add 1 tsp. of the oil and tilt the pan to coat the bottom evenly. Add about ½ cup prepared pancake batter to make a pancake about 6 to 8 inches in diameter.

Lay one-quarter of the shrimp, scallions, zucchini, carrots and chives on top of the batter. While the pancake is cooking, spoon a quarter of the beaten eggs over the pancake to fill in the spaces between the vegetables. After 3 to 5 minutes, when the egg mixture begins to set and the pancake bottom is well browned, turn the pancake over. Cook until browned, 3 to 4 more minutes, pressing down hard with a wide spatula to ensure that the batter cooks through. Slide onto a plate. Repeat with remaining oil, batter and vegetables.

Cut each pancake into wedges and serve with the dipping sauce on the side.

Serves 4.

375 CALORIES PER SERVING: 21 G PROTEIN, 12 G FAT, 42 G CARBOHYDRATE; 159 MG SODIUM; 204 MG CHOLESTEROL.

Sticky Rice with Peas

1   cup short-grain glutinous rice (*see* "The Well-Stocked Kitchen" *on page 221*) or basmati rice

½   tsp. salt

1   cup fresh or frozen peas (not thawed)

Rinse glutinous rice in a strainer under cold water, rubbing with your fingers to remove excess starch. (If using basmati rice, you do not need to rinse it.) Drain and transfer to a medium-sized saucepan. Add 1⅔ cups cold water and salt. Bring to a simmer over medium-high heat, stirring occasionally. As soon as the water simmers, reduce heat to low and cover the pan. Cook until nearly all the water has been absorbed, 8 to 12 minutes. Add peas and cook until all the water has been absorbed, 2 to 3 more minutes. Remove from the heat and let stand, covered, for 5 minutes.

   Serves 4.

200 CALORIES PER SERVING: 5 G PROTEIN, 0 G FAT, 43 G CARBOHYDRATE; 304 MG SODIUM; 0 MG CHOLESTEROL.

Strawberries with Ginger & Pine Nuts

1   Tbsp. pine nuts, coarsely chopped

1½   pts. strawberries, hulled and quartered

2   Tbsp. orange juice

1   Tbsp. chopped crystallized ginger or preserved stem ginger

2   tsp. sugar

In a small dry skillet over low heat, stir pine nuts until lightly toasted, about 3 minutes. Transfer to a medium-sized serving bowl; let cool briefly and add strawberries, orange juice, ginger and sugar, stirring to combine. Let stand for 10 minutes for flavors to blend.

   Serves 4.

45 CALORIES PER SERVING: 1 G PROTEIN, 2 G FAT, 8 G CARBOHYDRATE; 1 MG SODIUM; 0 MG CHOLESTEROL.

Salad on the Grill

MENU

....

*Grilled
Mediterranean
Vegetable Salad*

Garlic Croutons

*Macedoine of Melon
& Hazelnuts
with Ouzo*

(Anisette Toasts)

THIS MENU CONTAINS
505 CALORIES
PER SERVING WITH
30% OF CALORIES
FROM FAT.

Summer's harvest of vegetables is featured in this Mediterranean-inspired salad. Peasant-like and satisfying, it combines grilled eggplant, zucchini, tomatoes, fennel and onions with a fresh-tasting vinaigrette. Even the lemon slices are grilled; not only do they look great, they're a bracing taste experience. Alongside the salad, serve garlicky croutons, toasted on the grill and brushed with a pungent anchovy sauce. Dessert makes use of a ripe, fragrant melon in a simple *macedoine*; the term comes from Macedonia and has come to mean any fresh or cooked fruit, attractively cut and soaked or drizzled with a liqueur syrup. Here, we use Greek ouzo and sprinkle a few pretty hazelnuts on top. The anise flavor of the ouzo is echoed by the anisette toasts, which you can find at most supermarkets.

Grilled Mediterranean Vegetable Salad

DRESSING

- 2 plum tomatoes, cored, seeded and coarsely chopped
- 3 Tbsp. lemon juice
- 3 Tbsp. defatted reduced-sodium chicken stock
- 1½ Tbsp. olive oil, preferably extra-virgin
- 1 Tbsp. chopped fresh oregano or 1 tsp. dried oregano
  salt & freshly ground black pepper to taste

SALAD

- 1 small eggplant, cut into ¼-inch-thick rounds
- 2 small zucchini, trimmed and cut into ¼-inch-thick ovals
- 4 plum tomatoes, cored and cut in half lengthwise

1. *Make salad dressing.*

2. *Slice bread; make anchovy sauce.*

3. *Make macedoine.*

4. *Preheat grill.*

5. *Prepare salad vegetables.*

6. *Grill vegetables and bread.*

1	fennel bulb, trimmed and cut into 8 wedges
1	red onion, peeled and sliced into ¼-inch-thick slices (rings kept intact)
1	lemon, cut into ⅛-inch-thick rounds
¾	cup crumbled feta cheese, preferably imported (3 oz.)
8	imported black olives, preferably Kalamata, pitted and cut in half
	freshly ground black pepper to taste

To make salad dressing: In a blender or food processor, combine tomatoes, lemon juice, chicken stock, olive oil and oregano. Blend or process until smooth. Season with salt and pepper.

To make salad: Prepare a grill. Lightly oil grill rack and grill eggplant, zucchini, tomatoes, fennel, onions and lemon slices, in batches if necessary, until browned and tender; fennel will take 4 to 5 minutes per side, eggplant, zucchini and red onions 2 to 3 minutes per side, and tomatoes and lemons 1 to 2 minutes per side.

As the vegetables are done, transfer them to a large shallow serving dish. Toss gently with the dressing. Garnish with feta and black olives and a grinding of black pepper.

Serves 4.

178 CALORIES PER SERVING: 6 G PROTEIN, 12 G FAT, 17 G CARBOHYDRATE; 340 MG SODIUM; 19 MG CHOLESTEROL.

Garlic Croutons

1½	Tbsp. defatted reduced-sodium chicken stock
2	tsp. anchovy paste
1½	tsp. olive oil, preferably extra-virgin
8	½-inch-thick slices of French, Italian or sourdough bread
1	clove garlic, cut in half

Prepare a grill. In a small bowl, whisk together chicken stock, anchovy paste and olive oil. Set aside.

Grill bread slices, turning once, until well toasted on both sides, 2 to 3 minutes per side. Rub one side of each slice with the cut side of the garlic clove and brush with anchovy sauce.

Serves 4.

182 CALORIES PER SERVING: 6 G PROTEIN, 2 G FAT, 32 G CARBOHYDRATE; 379 MG SODIUM; 2 MG CHOLESTEROL.

Macedoine of Melon & Hazelnuts with Ouzo

1	Tbsp. chopped hazelnuts
½	cantaloupe, seeded
1	Tbsp. honey
1½	tsp. lemon juice
1½	tsp. ouzo or other anise-flavored liqueur

In a small dry skillet over low heat, stir hazelnuts until lightly toasted, about 3 minutes. Transfer to a plate to cool. With a knife, remove rind from cantaloupe and cut melon into 12 thin wedges.

In a medium-sized bowl, whisk together honey, lemon juice and ouzo. Add the melon, stirring gently to coat. Let the melon steep for 10 minutes, stirring occasionally.

To serve, arrange the melon on dessert plates. Spoon the marinade over the top and sprinkle with hazelnuts.

Serves 4.

45 CALORIES PER SERVING: 1 G PROTEIN, 1 G FAT, 8 G CARBOHYDRATE; 3 MG SODIUM; 0 MG CHOLESTEROL.

Autumn Menus

Chili Sans Carne - 118

Half-Hour Chili · Two-Pepper Corn Bread · Frosted Grapes

The Turkey-Cutlet Caper - 121

Turkey Piccata · Orzo & Toasted Barley · (Sliced Tomatoes) · Caramelized Apple Parfaits

A Sweet Way with Chicken - 125

North Country Braised Chicken · Green Beans with Shallot Dressing · (Whole-Wheat Rolls)
Rice Pudding with Dried Fruits

Robust Fish Roast - 128

Roasted Fish Catalán · (Steamed Zucchini or Broccoli) · Herbed White Bean Puree
Glazed Plum Tarts

Curry in a Hurry - 131

Shrimp & Coconut Milk Curry · Basmati Rice with Raisins & Cashews
Cucumber Salad · (Pomegranates)

Time for a Thick Soup - 135

Tomato & White Bean Soup · Sliced Fennel Salad · (French or Italian Bread)
Apple Butter Spice Cake

Mediterranean Holiday - 138

Eggplant, Lamb & Rice Casserole · Tzatziki · (Crusty Bread) · Apricot & Kumquat Compote

Chili Sans Carne

From chuck wagon to roadside diner to epicurean cook-off, chili has been an all-American favorite for well over a century. But the problem for the short-order cook—or overextended professional—is that good chili usually takes at least one hour of slow simmering. Half-Hour Chili, however, is easy to prepare, meatless and full-flavored. Bulgur replaces the beef for texture and satisfying body. A low-fat but moist corn bread speckled with red and green peppers accompanies the chili. Try to use stone-ground cornmeal; it contains bits of the outer bran layer, making a more nutritious and tastier corn bread. Frosted grapes make a whimsical, fantastically easy conclusion to the meal.

Half-Hour Chili
....

1	Tbsp. vegetable oil, preferably canola oil
3	onions, chopped
1	carrot, chopped
1	Tbsp. finely chopped jalapeño pepper
2	cloves garlic, finely chopped
3-4	tsp. chili powder
1	tsp. ground cumin
1	28-oz. can and one 14-oz. can tomatoes, chopped, with juices
1	tsp. brown sugar
2	15-oz. cans red kidney beans, drained and rinsed
⅓	cup bulgur (*see "The Well-Stocked Kitchen" on page 221*)
½	cup nonfat plain yogurt
⅓	cup chopped scallions
¼	cup chopped fresh parsley

In a Dutch oven or a large saucepan, heat oil over medium heat. Add onions, carrots, jalapeños, garlic, chili powder and cumin. Sauté until the onions and carrots are soft, 5 to 7 minutes.

Add tomatoes with their juice and sugar; cook for 5 minutes over high heat. Reduce heat to low; stir in beans and bulgur. Simmer the chili until thickened, about 15 minutes.

Serve with yogurt, scallions and parsley on the side.

Serves 4.

412 CALORIES PER SERVING: 21 G PROTEIN, 6 G FAT, 75 G CARBOHYDRATE; 810 MG SO-DIUM; 2 MG CHOLESTEROL.

Two-Pepper Corn Bread

1 cup buttermilk
1 large egg
1 Tbsp. vegetable oil, preferably canola oil
1 Tbsp. honey
1 red bell pepper, cored, seeded and finely chopped
1 4-oz. can chopped green chilies, drained
1 cup all-purpose white flour
¾ cup yellow cornmeal, preferably stone-ground
2 tsp. baking powder
½ tsp. salt
½ tsp. baking soda

Preheat oven to 450 degrees F. Lightly oil an 8-inch square baking pan or coat it with nonstick cooking spray.

In a medium-sized bowl, whisk together buttermilk, egg, oil and honey. Stir in bell peppers and chilies.

In a large bowl, stir together flour, cornmeal, baking powder, salt and baking soda. Pour in the buttermilk mixture and stir just until the dry ingredients are moistened: do not overmix. Pour the batter into the prepared pan, spreading to the edges.

Timetable

1. Preheat oven to 450 degrees F.

2. Freeze grapes.

3. Mix and bake corn bread.

4. Make chili.

Bake for 25 minutes, or until golden and a toothpick inserted in the center comes out clean. Let cool on a wire rack for 5 minutes before cutting into squares and serving.

Serves 4.

288 CALORIES PER SERVING: 9 G PROTEIN, 6 G FAT, 49 G CARBOHYDRATE; 1,004 MG SODIUM; 54 MG CHOLESTEROL.

Frosted Grapes

1½ lbs. red or green seedless grapes

Wash grapes and pat dry. Place in the freezer for 45 minutes. Remove from the freezer and let sit for 2 minutes before serving.

Serves 4.

107 CALORIES PER SERVING: 1 G PROTEIN, 1 G FAT, 29 G CARBOHYDRATE; 3 MG SODIUM; 0 MG CHOLESTEROL.

The Turkey-Cutlet Caper

A sprightly Turkey Piccata is the focal point of this light, early-autumn meal; a pair of grains in Orzo & Toasted Barley pilaf and some perfectly ripe sliced tomatoes fill out the plate. For dessert, there is a stylish confection of sliced apples braised in a caramelized sugar syrup, layered in parfait glasses with vanilla yogurt. *Piccata* is the northern Italian term for a veal cutlet. In this version, the fat and the expense have been cut by substituting turkey for veal, and the marriage of the flavors between the white breast meat and the piquant, lemony sauce with capers and parsley is delightful.

Turkey Piccata

1	lemon
⅓	cup all-purpose white flour
½	tsp. salt
½	tsp. freshly ground black pepper, plus more to taste
4	turkey cutlets (about 1 lb.), each cutlet cut in half
2	tsp. olive oil
1	clove garlic, finely chopped
½	cup defatted reduced-sodium chicken stock
1	Tbsp. capers, rinsed
½	tsp. sugar
2	tsp. butter
1	Tbsp. chopped fresh parsley

With a sharp knife, remove skin and white pith from lemon and discard. Working over a bowl to catch the juice, cut the lemon segments from their surrounding membranes. Chop the segments coarsely and reserve

MENU

Turkey Piccata

*Orzo &
Toasted Barley*

(Sliced Tomatoes)

*Caramelized
Apple Parfaits*

THIS MENU CONTAINS
780 CALORIES
PER SERVING WITH
14% OF CALORIES
FROM FAT.

with the juice.

Combine flour, salt and ½ tsp. pepper in a shallow dish. Lightly dredge cutlets in the flour mixture and pat off excess.

Heat oil in a large nonstick skillet over medium-high heat. Add the cutlets to the skillet and cook until the outside is golden brown and the interior is no longer pink, 2 to 3 minutes per side. Transfer to a platter and keep warm.

Add garlic to the skillet and cook, stirring, for several seconds. Pour in chicken stock and bring to a boil. Cook, stirring, for 1 minute. Add the reserved lemon segments and juice, capers and sugar; cook for 30 seconds more. Add butter, swirling the skillet to melt the butter.

Spoon the sauce over the reserved turkey, sprinkle with parsley and pepper.

Serves 4.

220 CALORIES PER SERVING: 27 G PROTEIN, 7 G FAT, 11 G CARBOHYDRATE; 383 MG SODIUM; 64 MG CHOLESTEROL.

Orzo & Toasted Barley

1	tsp. vegetable oil, preferably canola oil
1	cup quick-cooking barley
1	clove garlic, finely chopped
2½	cups defatted reduced-sodium chicken stock
½	cup orzo (*see* "The Well-Stocked Kitchen" *on page 221*)
1	Tbsp. chopped fresh thyme or 1 tsp. dried thyme leaves
¼	cup chopped chives or scallion greens
	salt & freshly ground black pepper to taste

In a medium-sized heavy saucepan, heat oil over medium heat. Add barley and cook, stirring, until golden and toasted, about 5 minutes. Add garlic and stir for 1 minute more. Pour in chicken stock and bring to a boil. Add orzo and thyme. Stir once, reduce heat to low, cover and simmer for 10 minutes.

Remove from the heat and let rest for 5 minutes to absorb any re-

Timetable

1. *Drain yogurt and toast walnuts for parfaits.*

2. *Cook apples for parfaits.*

3. *Make orzo & barley.*

4. *Assemble parfaits.*

5. *Make turkey piccata.*

maining liquid. Stir in chives or scallion greens. Season with salt and pepper.

Serves 4.

224 CALORIES PER SERVING: 8 G PROTEIN, 2 G FAT, 44 G CARBOHYDRATE; 7 MG SODIUM; 0 MG CHOLESTEROL.

Caramelized Apple Parfaits

1 Tbsp. chopped walnuts (optional)
2 cups low-fat vanilla yogurt
⅔ cup sugar
2 tsp. butter
4 large baking apples, such as Rome, Golden Delicious or Cortland, peeled, cored and thinly sliced
1 Tbsp. fresh lemon juice

In a small dry skillet over low heat, stir walnuts until lightly toasted, about 3 minutes. Transfer to a plate to cool.

Line a sieve with cheesecloth or coffee filters and set it over a bowl. Spoon in yogurt and let drain for about 30 minutes.

Meanwhile, in a medium-sized heavy saucepan, stir together sugar and 2 Tbsp. water. Bring to a boil, stirring to dissolve the sugar. Cook, without stirring, until the syrup turns deep amber, about 5 minutes. (Do not let the syrup burn.) Remove from the heat, add butter and swirl the pan until the butter has melted. Add apples and lemon juice. Return the pan to the stovetop, cover and cook over low heat for 5 minutes. Uncover, and cook, stirring occasionally, until the apples are tender and the juice has thickened slightly, 15 to 20 minutes. Let cool for 5 minutes.

Spoon alternating layers of the caramelized apples and drained yogurt into 4 parfait or wine glasses. Sprinkle walnuts over the top, if desired.

Serves 4.

311 CALORIES PER SERVING: 6 G PROTEIN, 3 G FAT, 71 G CARBOHYDRATE; 92 MG SODIUM; 8 MG CHOLESTEROL.

A Sweet Way with Chicken

The sweet earthiness of rutabagas and onions blends with moist chicken breasts, pears and cider for an entrée that captures and distills the essence of autumn. Alongside the chicken, serve a warm salad of steamed green beans, tossed with a tart Dijon-mustard dressing. The rich and old-fashioned dessert is rice pudding studded with ruby-red dried cranberries and golden apricots. A medium-grain rice, such as Italian arborio, makes the pudding creamier, because it has a higher starch content.

North Country Braised Chicken

2	Tbsp. all-purpose white flour
4	4-oz. boneless, skinless chicken breasts, fat trimmed
1	tsp. vegetable oil, preferably canola oil
1	onion, coarsely chopped
¾	cup apple cider or juice
1	small rutabaga, peeled and cut into ¼-inch-by-2-inch julienne (about 4 cups)
1	cup defatted reduced-sodium chicken stock
2	firm ripe pears, such as Anjou, Bosc or Comice
2	Tbsp. fresh lemon juice
1½	tsp. chopped fresh thyme or ½ tsp. dried thyme leaves salt & freshly ground black pepper to taste

Place flour on a plate and dredge both sides of chicken breasts to coat, shaking off excess. Reserve unused flour.

In a large nonstick skillet, heat oil over high heat. Add chicken and sauté until golden, about 2 minutes per side. Remove to a plate and set aside.

MENU

North Country Braised Chicken

Green Beans with Shallot Dressing

(Whole-Wheat Rolls)

Rice Pudding with Dried Fruits

THIS MENU CONTAINS
664 CALORIES
PER SERVING WITH
9% OF CALORIES
FROM FAT.

Timetable

....

1. *Trim green beans.*

2. *Start rice pudding.*

3. *Make chicken.*

4. *Add fruit to rice pudding.*

5. *Steam green beans; make dressing.*

Reduce heat to medium-low and add onions. Stir until lightly browned, about 2 minutes. Add the reserved flour and stir 1 minute more. Gradually add apple cider or juice and stir until thickened, about 2 minutes. Add rutabagas and chicken stock. Bring to a simmer, reduce heat to low and cover. Cook until the rutabaga is tender, 15 to 20 minutes.

Meanwhile, peel and core pears; cut into ½-inch dice. Transfer to a small bowl and stir in lemon juice and thyme. Add to the cooked rutabaga mixture and season with salt and pepper. Lay the reserved chicken on top and cover the pan. Cook until the chicken is no longer pink in the center and the pears are tender, 5 to 6 minutes more.

Serves 4.

273 CALORIES PER SERVING: 29 G PROTEIN, 4 G FAT, 30 G CARBOHYDRATE; 84 MG SODIUM; 71 MG CHOLESTEROL.

Green Beans with Shallot Dressing

1   lb. green beans, trimmed
1   large shallot, finely chopped
2   Tbsp. defatted reduced-sodium chicken stock
1   Tbsp. red-wine vinegar
1   tsp. whole-grain Dijon mustard
    salt & freshly ground black pepper to taste

Place green beans in a steamer basket over boiling water, cover and steam until tender. (*Alternatively, microwave beans with ¼ cup water, covered, on high power for 6 to 8 minutes, or until tender, stirring once. Drain.*)

In a serving bowl, whisk together shallots, chicken stock, vinegar and mustard. Toss the hot beans with the dressing, season with salt and pepper and serve immediately.

Serves 4.

38 CALORIES PER SERVING: 2 G PROTEIN, 0 G FAT, 9 G CARBOHYDRATE; 10 MG SODIUM; 0 MG CHOLESTEROL.

Rice Pudding with Dried Fruits

- ½ cup medium-grain rice, such as Italian arborio (*see "The Well-Stocked Kitchen" on page 221*)
- ⅓ cup sugar
- ½ tsp. cornstarch
- pinch of salt
- 2¼ cups 1% milk
- ¼ cup dried cranberries
- ¼ cup chopped dried apricots
- 2 tsp. pure vanilla extract
- freshly grated nutmeg

Conventional Method: In a medium-sized heavy saucepan, whisk together rice, sugar, cornstarch and salt. Gradually stir in milk. Bring to a simmer over high heat, stirring constantly. Reduce heat to low and simmer slowly, stirring often, until the rice is tender and the pudding is creamy, about 20 minutes. Remove from heat and stir in cranberries, apricots and vanilla. Cover the pan and let sit for 10 minutes, or until ready to serve.

Microwave Method: Whisk together rice, sugar, cornstarch and salt in a 3-qt. or larger casserole. Gradually stir in milk. Cover with lid or vented plastic wrap and microwave on high power for 5 minutes, or until the mixture is simmering. Stir, cover and microwave on medium power (50 percent) for 30 minutes, or until the rice is tender and the pudding is creamy. Stir in cranberries, apricots and vanilla. Cover and let stand for 10 minutes, or until ready to serve.

Spoon into individual bowls and top with freshly grated nutmeg.

Serves 4.

272 CALORIES PER SERVING: 7 G PROTEIN, 2 G FAT, 57 G CARBOHYDRATE; 202 MG SODIUM; 5 MG CHOLESTEROL.

Robust Fish Roast

MENU

....

*Roasted Fish
Catalán*

*(Steamed Zucchini
or Broccoli)*

*Herbed
White Bean Puree*

*Glazed
Plum Tarts*

THIS MENU CONTAINS
607 CALORIES
PER SERVING WITH
19% OF CALORIES
FROM FAT.

From Mexico to Morocco, many coastal countries offer some version of this dish. The firm flesh of the fish is kept moist by the fresh vegetables during roasting. It is a versatile dish; you could add capers, roasted peppers, sun-dried tomatoes or potatoes. The white bean puree is a rich, creamy complement to the fish. To round out the meal, add a simple steamed vegetable, such as zucchini or broccoli. For dessert, these fast and pretty plum tarts make use of a round of lightly buttered bread for a quick crust. The fruit is scented with cinnamon and the warm tarts are topped with a spoonful of creamy vanilla yogurt.

Roasted Fish Catalán

1   lb. thick-cut, firm-fleshed fish fillets (halibut, mahi-mahi, monkfish)
    salt & freshly ground black pepper to taste
2   tsp. olive oil
1   large onion, thinly sliced
3   Tbsp. dry white or red wine
2   cloves garlic, finely chopped
1   14-oz. can whole tomatoes, drained and coarsely chopped
8   black olives, preferably Kalamata, pitted and coarsely chopped
¼   tsp. dried oregano
¼   tsp. grated orange zest

Preheat oven to 450 degrees F. Cut fish into 4 serving pieces and season with salt and pepper. Arrange in a single layer in a 10-inch pie plate or baking dish.

In a large nonstick skillet, heat oil over medium-high heat. Add onions and sauté until lightly browned, about 5 minutes. Add wine and garlic and simmer for 30 seconds. Stir in tomatoes, olives, oregano and orange zest. Season with salt and pepper. Spoon mixture over the fish.

Bake for 15 minutes, or until the fish is opaque in the center.

Serves 4.

162 CALORIES PER SERVING: 21 G PROTEIN, 4 G FAT, 8 G CARBOHYDRATE; 283 MG SODIUM; 47 MG CHOLESTEROL.

Herbed White Bean Puree

- 3 cloves garlic, peeled and cut in half
- 2 15-oz. cans cannellini or great Northern beans, drained and rinsed
- 2 Tbsp. finely chopped fresh parsley
- 1 Tbsp. olive oil, preferably extra-virgin
- 1 tsp. finely chopped fresh sage or ½ tsp. dried rubbed sage
  salt & freshly ground black pepper to taste

Fill a large saucepan with cold water, add garlic and bring to a boil over high heat. Add beans and return to a boil. Reserve ½ cup of the cooking liquid, then drain beans and garlic in a strainer or colander.

Transfer the beans and garlic to a food processor. Add parsley, olive oil and sage; puree the mixture, adding enough of the reserved cooking liquid, if necessary, to make a thick puree. Return to the saucepan and heat through. Season with salt and pepper.

Serves 4.

235 CALORIES PER SERVING: 14 G PROTEIN, 4 G FAT, 37 G CARBOHYDRATE; 10 MG SODIUM; 0 MG CHOLESTEROL.

Timetable

1. *Preheat oven to 450 degrees F.*

2. *Cook plums and prepare bread rounds for tarts.*

3. *Prepare zucchini or broccoli for steaming.*

4. *Make fish.*

5. *While fish bakes, make bean puree and steam zucchini or broccoli.*

6. *Assemble and bake tarts.*

Glazed Plum Tarts

6 plums, cut in half, pitted and thinly sliced (2 cups)

¼ cup sugar

¼ tsp. ground cinnamon

4 pieces very thinly sliced white bread, preferably Pepperidge Farm, cut into 4-inch rounds

1 Tbsp. melted butter

¼ cup low-fat vanilla yogurt

Place rack in upper third of oven; preheat to 450 degrees F.

In a medium-sized saucepan, combine plums, sugar and cinnamon. Cook over medium heat, stirring frequently, until the plums are tender and the juices have thickened, 5 to 7 minutes.

Meanwhile, place bread rounds on a baking sheet and brush with melted butter. Spoon the plum mixture over each bread round, so that all the bread is covered.

Bake the tarts for 6 to 8 minutes, or until the bread is crisp. Serve topped with a dollop of yogurt.

Serves 4.

201 CALORIES PER SERVING: 3 G PROTEIN, 5 G FAT, 39 G CARBOHYDRATE; 157 MG SODIUM; 9 MG CHOLESTEROL.

Curry in a Hurry

Rich and exotic, this fragrant and beautiful menu is a good one to save for company. Although the Thai-style curry is flavored with coconut milk, this version is made considerably lower in saturated fat by replacing some of the coconut milk with evaporated skim milk. Alongside is a simple rice pilaf, textured with toasted cashews or almonds and sweetened with golden raisins. Use one of the aromatic long-grain rices. Jasmine rice, originally from Thailand, is sweetly perfumed and delicate. Basmati, from the foothills of the Himalayas, has a nuttier flavor and scent. The slightly hot and sweet cucumber salad provides a cool accompaniment. For dessert, try pomegranates; they are in season now through the end of the year.

Shrimp & Coconut Milk Curry

¼ cup unsweetened coconut milk (*see* "The Well-Stocked Kitchen" *on page 221*)

2 tsp. cornstarch

1 tsp. vegetable oil, preferably canola oil

1 onion, chopped

1 red bell pepper, cored, seeded and chopped

2 cloves garlic, finely chopped

1 jalapeño pepper, seeded and finely chopped

4 tsp. curry powder, preferably Madras (*see* "The Well-Stocked Kitchen" *on page 221*)

1 tsp. ground cumin

1 tsp. ground coriander

1 cup evaporated skim milk

THIS MENU CONTAINS 646 CALORIES PER SERVING WITH 17% OF CALORIES FROM FAT.

1   lb. large shrimp, peeled and deveined

4   tsp. fresh lime juice

¼   cup chopped fresh cilantro

    salt & freshly ground black pepper to taste

In a small bowl, whisk together coconut milk and cornstarch until smooth; set aside.

Heat oil in a large heavy saucepan over medium heat. Add onions and bell peppers; sauté until softened, about 5 minutes. Add garlic, jalapeños, curry powder, cumin and coriander; sauté until aromatic, about 2 minutes more. Reduce heat to low and stir in reserved coconut milk mixture and evaporated skim milk. Bring to a simmer, stirring. Cook for 5 minutes, stirring often. Add shrimp and cook, stirring occasionally, until they are pink and curled, 7 to 10 minutes. Remove from heat and stir in lime juice and cilantro; season with salt and pepper.

Serves 4.

251 CALORIES PER SERVING: 30 G PROTEIN, 7 G FAT, 17 G CARBOHYDRATE; 251 MG SODIUM; 178 MG CHOLESTEROL.

Basmati Rice with Raisins & Cashews

················

1   tsp. vegetable oil, preferably canola oil

3   Tbsp. coarsely chopped raw cashews or almonds

1   cup rice, preferably basmati (*see* "The Well-Stocked Kitchen" *on page 221*), rinsed with cold water

½   cup golden raisins

½   tsp. salt

¼   tsp. freshly ground black pepper

2   scallions, trimmed and thinly sliced

Conventional Method: Heat oil in a medium-sized pan over medium-high heat. Add nuts and sauté until toasted, about 1 minute. Add rice, raisins, salt, pepper and 1½ cups water; bring to a boil. Reduce heat to low, cover and cook until the rice is tender and all the water is absorbed,

15 to 20 minutes. With a fork, fluff the rice and stir in scallions.

Microwave Method: Toss nuts with oil in a 2½-qt. casserole. Microwave on high for 2 to 3 minutes, or until nuts are golden. Add rice, raisins, salt, pepper and 1½ cups water. Cover casserole with a lid or vented plastic wrap and microwave on high power for 5 minutes. Stir once, cover and microwave on medium power (50 percent), without stirring, for 10 minutes more, or until rice is cooked. Let stand, covered, for 5 minutes. With a fork, fluff the rice and stir in scallions.

Serves 4.

270 CALORIES PER SERVING: 5 G PROTEIN, 5 G FAT, 53 G CARBOHYDRATE; 272 MG SODIUM; 0 MG CHOLESTEROL.

Cucumber Salad

2 cucumbers
1 Tbsp. rice-wine or distilled white vinegar
¼ tsp. sugar
   cayenne pepper to taste
   salt & freshly ground black pepper to taste

Peel cucumbers and cut in half lengthwise. With a teaspoon, scrape out and discard seeds. Cut the cucumbers crosswise into ¼-inch slices.

Place in a medium-sized bowl along with vinegar, sugar and cayenne. Toss to combine. Season with salt and pepper. Refrigerate until serving time.

Serves 4.

21 CALORIES PER SERVING: 1 G PROTEIN, 0 G FAT, 5 G CARBOHYDRATE; 3 MG SODIUM; 0 MG CHOLESTEROL.

Time for a Thick Soup

O n a crisp fall evening, a hearty soup nourishes the soul as well as the body. This one is thick with pureed white beans, roasted tomatoes and garlic. Roasting concentrates and intensifies the flavor of the tomatoes, sweetens and mellows the garlic. Fresh herbs are called for, and they're well worth the chopping time because their lively flavor adds so much to this quickly made meal. The fennel salad can either be served with the soup or alone as the meal's opening course. After you've perfumed and warmed the house with the aromas of roasting tomatoes and garlic, add the scents of apples and spice as you make this dark, moist cake, reminiscent of gingerbread.

Tomato & White Bean Soup

- 2½ lbs. plum tomatoes (about 15-18 small tomatoes)
- 8 unpeeled cloves garlic
- 1½ Tbsp. olive oil
  - salt & freshly ground black pepper to taste
- 1 19-oz. can cannellini beans, drained and rinsed
- 2½ cups defatted reduced-sodium chicken stock
- ¼ cup dry vermouth
- 1 Tbsp. chopped fresh sage or 1¼ tsp. dried rubbed sage
- 1½ tsp. chopped fresh thyme or ½ tsp. dried thyme leaves
- 1 tsp. sugar
  - salt & freshly ground black pepper to taste

Place racks in the middle and lower third of the oven; preheat to 450 degrees F. Slice stem end from tomatoes, quarter them lengthwise and divide them between 2 baking sheets. Scatter garlic on top. Drizzle the

Timetable

. . . .

1. *Preheat oven to 450 degrees F.*

2. *Prepare and roast tomatoes and garlic.*

3. *Assemble rest of soup ingredients.*

4. *Lower oven to 350 degrees F.*

5. *Mix and bake cake.*

6. *Slice fennel; make dressing.*

7. *Finish soup.*

tomatoes with the olive oil and toss to combine, spreading the tomatoes out in a single layer. Sprinkle with salt and pepper. Roast the tomatoes, switching the pans midway, for 20 to 25 minutes, or until the tomato skins are browned and the garlic is soft. Cool for 5 minutes.

Slip the soft garlic pulp from the skins and place in a food processor, discarding the skins. Add the tomatoes with their skins, scraping any juices from the bottom of the baking sheet. Add ½ cup of the beans, reserving the rest. Puree the mixture until smooth. Transfer it to a large saucepan. Add the reserved beans, chicken stock, vermouth, sage, thyme and sugar. Bring to a simmer over medium-high heat and cook for 2 minutes, stirring occasionally. Season with salt and pepper.

Makes 6 cups.

Serves 4.

300 CALORIES PER SERVING: 15 G PROTEIN, 6 G FAT, 47 G CARBOHYDRATE; 35 MG SODIUM; 0 MG CHOLESTEROL.

Sliced Fennel Salad

. . . .

1 fennel bulb
1 Tbsp. olive oil, preferably extra-virgin
1 Tbsp. lemon juice
⅛ tsp. salt
   freshly ground black pepper to taste

Trim base from fennel bulb. Remove and discard the fennel stalks; reserve some of the feathery leaves for garnish. Pull off and discard any discolored parts from the bulb. Stand the bulb upright and cut vertically into very thin slices. Arrange the slices on 4 salad plates.

In a small bowl, whisk together oil, lemon juice and salt. Drizzle the mixture over the fennel and garnish with a grinding of black pepper and a few fennel leaves.

Serves 4.

34 CALORIES PER SERVING: 0 G PROTEIN, 3 G FAT, 1 G CARBOHYDRATE; 86 MG SODIUM; 0 MG CHOLESTEROL.

Apple Butter Spice Cake

1 Tbsp. butter
1 cup apple butter
¾ cup packed light brown sugar
3 Tbsp. vegetable oil, preferably canola oil
½ cup raisins
½ cup buttermilk
1 large egg
2 tsp. pure vanilla extract
2 cups plus 2 Tbsp. all-purpose white flour
2 tsp. baking soda
2 tsp. ground cinnamon
2 tsp. ground ginger
1 tsp. ground allspice
¼ tsp. salt

Preheat oven to 350 degrees F. Lightly oil an 8-inch square cake pan or coat it with nonstick cooking spray.

In a small saucepan, melt butter over medium heat; swirl the pan until the butter turns a nutty brown, about 60 seconds. Pour into a medium-sized bowl. Add apple butter, brown sugar (breaking up any lumps) and oil and whisk until smooth. Add raisins, buttermilk, egg and vanilla; mix well. Add flour, baking soda, cinnamon, ginger, allspice and salt; whisk until just combined.

Turn the batter out into the baking dish and bake for 35 to 40 minutes, or until a knife inserted in the center comes out clean. Let cool in the pan on a rack for 10 minutes. Cut into squares and serve warm.

Serves 9.

337 CALORIES PER SERVING: 5 G PROTEIN, 7 G FAT, 65 G CARBOHYDRATE; 283 MG SODIUM; 28 MG CHOLESTEROL.

Mediterranean Holiday

MENU

....

*Eggplant,
Lamb & Rice
Casserole*

Tzatziki

(Crusty Bread)

*Apricot
& Kumquat
Compote*

THIS MENU CONTAINS
702 CALORIES, WITH
19% CALORIES
FROM FAT.

The innate wholesomeness of the Mediterranean diet—with its preponderance of vegetables, grains and fruits and its sparing use of meat—makes the creation of a balanced, healthful menu an easy task. The focal point of this quick supper is an Eggplant, Lamb & Rice Casserole, flavored with feta cheese, oregano, thyme and a bit of cinnamon. *Tzatziki*, a tart salad of yogurt and cucumbers, fills out the plate along with thick slices of warm bread. The meal ends with a mixture of dried and fresh fruit, a colorful compote of apricots, kumquats and pistachios.

Eggplant, Lamb & Rice Casserole

....

- 2 lbs. eggplant (2 large), cut in half lengthwise
- ½ lb. lean ground lamb or beef
- 2 tsp. olive oil
- 2 onions, chopped
- 1 red bell pepper, cored, seeded and chopped
- 2 cloves garlic, finely chopped
- 1 14½-oz. can tomatoes, with juice
- 2 tsp. dried oregano
- ½ tsp. dried thyme leaves
- ½ tsp. ground cinnamon
- ¼ tsp. ground cloves
- 1 cup long-grain white rice
- 1 14½-oz. can defatted reduced-sodium beef broth
  salt & freshly ground black pepper to taste
- ½ cup crumbled feta cheese, preferably imported (2 oz.)

Preheat oven to 450 degrees F. Place eggplant halves, cut-side down, in a roasting pan. Add water to a depth of ½ inch. Bake for 20 to 25 minutes, or until tender; set aside. Reduce oven temperature to 400 degrees F.

While the eggplant is roasting, heat a large Dutch oven over medium-high heat. Add ground lamb or beef and cook, breaking up the meat with a wooden spoon, until browned, 3 to 5 minutes. Transfer to a colander and drain off the fat. Set aside.

Add oil to the Dutch oven and heat over medium heat. Add onions and cook until golden, about 5 minutes. Add red peppers and garlic and cook for 2 minutes more. Stir in tomatoes and their juice, oregano, thyme, cinnamon and cloves. Simmer, breaking up the tomatoes with a wooden spoon, until the mixture has thickened slightly, 3 to 5 minutes.

Scoop out the eggplant flesh and chop coarsely. Stir rice, beef broth, the chopped eggplant and the reserved lamb or beef into the tomato mixture; bring to a simmer. Cover the pan and place it in the oven. Bake for 30 to 35 minutes, or until the rice is tender and the liquid has been absorbed. Season with salt and pepper. Dot with feta and serve.

Serves 4.

408 CALORIES PER SERVING: 19 G PROTEIN, 12 G FAT, 58 G CARBOHYDRATE; 697 MG SODIUM; 55 MG CHOLESTEROL.

Tzatziki

1 large or 2 small cucumbers, peeled, cut in half and seeded
1 clove garlic, peeled
¼ tsp. salt
½ cup low-fat plain yogurt
2 Tbsp. chopped fresh mint or 2 tsp. dried
  freshly ground black pepper to taste

Coarsely grate cucumbers and gently squeeze by hand to remove excess liquid; set aside.

Timetable

....

1. Preheat oven to 450 degrees F.

2. Prepare and start baking casserole.

3. Make apricot compote.

4. Make cucumber salad.

On a cutting board, chop garlic coarsely, and sprinkle with salt. Using the flat side of a knife, work the salted garlic into a paste.

In a medium-sized bowl, whisk together the garlic paste, yogurt and mint. Stir in the reserved cucumbers. Season with salt and pepper to taste.

Serves 4.

41 CALORIES PER SERVING: 2 G PROTEIN, 1 G FAT, 7 G CARBOHYDRATE; 157 MG SODIUM; 2 MG CHOLESTEROL.

Apricot & Kumquat Compote

If you cannot find kumquats, increase the quantity of apricots to 1½ cups and add a strip of lemon peel and a strip of orange peel to the cooking liquid.

- 1 cup dried apricots (6 oz.)
- 6 fresh kumquats, sliced and seeded
- ¾ cup sugar
- 1 cinnamon stick
- 2 Tbsp. unsalted shelled pistachios, skinned and coarsely chopped

In a medium-sized saucepan, combine apricots, kumquats, sugar, cinnamon stick and 1¼ cups water. Bring to a simmer over low heat. Cover and cook until the fruit is tender, 15 to 20 minutes.

Remove the cinnamon stick. Serve sprinkled with pistachios.

Serves 4.

253 CALORIES PER SERVING: 2 G PROTEIN, 2 G FAT, 62 G CARBOHYDRATE; 6 MG SODIUM; 0 MG CHOLESTEROL.

A Southern Porch Supper

A folksy, Southern-inspired supper, this meal includes pork in barbecue sauce and a salad with black-eyed peas. Lean and tender pork tenderloin is rubbed with black pepper, then seared in a skillet before being brushed with a piquant jalapeño-molasses sauce and roasted. In the salad of artichoke hearts and black-eyed peas tossed with chopped red onions, caraway seeds are a surprising but tasty addition; they marry well with the slightly smoky flavor of the peas. The refreshing dessert combines orange and lemon juice, sugar and cinnamon with rounds of fresh navel oranges—which start arriving in the stores in the late fall.

MENU
....

*Pork Tenderloin
Southern Style*

*Black-Eyed Pea
& Artichoke Salad*

(French Bread)

*Cinnamon
Oranges*

THIS MENU CONTAINS
699 CALORIES
PER SERVING WITH
15% OF CALORIES
FROM FAT.

Pork Tenderloin Southern Style

- 2 tsp. olive oil
- ½ small onion, finely chopped
- 1 jalapeño pepper, seeded and finely chopped
- 1 clove garlic, finely chopped
- ¼ cup molasses
- ¼ cup cider vinegar
- 2 Tbsp. Dijon mustard
- 2 tsp. reduced-sodium soy sauce
- 2 ¾-lb. pork tenderloins, trimmed of fat
  freshly ground black pepper to taste

Preheat oven to 425 degrees F. In a medium-sized saucepan, heat 1 tsp. of the oil over medium heat. Add onions, jalapeños and garlic; sauté until softened, 2 to 3 minutes. Add molasses, vinegar, mustard and soy sauce; reduce heat to low and simmer, stirring occasionally, until quite thick, about 7 minutes.

[handwritten notes: very tender, good, cooking melted, we might like different mixture better]

Rub tenderloins generously with black pepper. Heat the remaining 1 tsp. oil in a medium-sized ovenproof skillet over medium-high heat. Add the tenderloins and cook, turning, until well browned on all sides, 2 to 3 minutes.

Brush the pork generously with some of the barbecue sauce. Place the skillet in the oven and roast for 7 minutes. Turn over the tenderloins and brush them with remaining sauce and roast for 7 to 8 minutes more, or until the internal temperature is 160 degrees F. Let the pork rest for 5 minutes. Carve into ¾-inch-thick slices and serve.

Serves 6.

232 CALORIES PER SERVING: 26 G PROTEIN, 7 G FAT, 18 G CARBOHYDRATE; 197 MG SODIUM; 79 MG CHOLESTEROL.

Black-Eyed Pea & Artichoke Salad

1	9-oz. pkg. frozen artichoke hearts, thawed
2	16-oz. cans black-eyed peas, drained and rinsed
½	cup chopped red onion
2	Tbsp. balsamic vinegar
1½	Tbsp. olive oil, preferably extra-virgin
1	tsp. Worcestershire sauce
½	tsp. caraway seeds, lightly crushed
	salt & freshly ground black pepper to taste
	red leaf lettuce

Squeeze any excess moisture from thawed artichoke hearts and cut each quarter in half. Place the artichokes in a medium-sized bowl, along with black-eyed peas, onions, vinegar, oil, Worcestershire sauce and caraway seeds. Toss thoroughly. Season with salt and pepper. Serve on lettuce leaves.

Serves 6.

237 CALORIES PER SERVING: 13 G PROTEIN, 4 G FAT, 39 G CARBOHYDRATE; 140 MG SODIUM; 0 MG CHOLESTEROL.

Timetable

1. Preheat oven to 425 degrees F.

2. Thaw artichokes under warm running water or in microwave.

3. Make barbecue sauce.

4. Finish salad.

5. Brown pork; put in oven.

6. Slice oranges; mix sauce.

Cinnamon Oranges

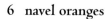

6 navel oranges
3 Tbsp. orange juice
3 Tbsp. lemon juice
3 Tbsp. sugar
½ tsp. ground cinnamon

With a very sharp knife, remove rind and white pith from oranges. Cut each orange into 5 or 6 slices and arrange in circles on individual dessert plates.

In a small bowl, whisk together orange juice, lemon juice, sugar and cinnamon; spoon over the orange slices.

Serves 6.

90 CALORIES PER SERVING: 1 G PROTEIN, 0 G FAT, 23 G CARBOHYDRATE; 1 MG SODIUM; 0 MG CHOLESTEROL.

Pumpkin in a New Light

Indian summer brings more than fiery leaves and afternoon haze; there's the end-of-summer vegetable bounty as well. In this meal, we make use of pumpkins, apples and pears. The curry is West African-inspired, and the rich-fleshed pumpkin is a great natural thickener. The curry is paired with a bulgur-and-chickpea pilaf, which can be made vegetarian by using water instead of beef stock. Bulgur wheat kernels have already been steamed, dried and cracked, so cooking time is minimal. Delicious and slightly mysterious, the warm poached pears for dessert are seasoned with bay leaves. The tart cherries are a pretty counterpoint to the mellow pears and the white wine-based poaching liquid reduces to form a lovely rosy sauce.

Pumpkin & Tomato Curry

- 1 Tbsp. olive oil
- 2 lbs. pumpkin or buttercup squash, peeled and cut into 1-inch cubes (4 cups)
- 1 large onion, thinly sliced
- 2 small tomatoes, cored, seeded and diced
- 3 Tbsp. curry powder, preferably Madras (*see* "The Well-Stocked Kitchen" *on page 221*)

  salt & freshly ground black pepper to taste

  nonfat plain yogurt for garnish

In a Dutch oven, heat oil over medium-high heat Add pumpkin or squash and cook, stirring occasionally, for 3 minutes. Add onions and cook, stirring frequently, for 4 minutes more. Add tomatoes, curry powder and 2½ cups water; bring to a boil.

MENU

Pumpkin & Tomato Curry

Bulgur-Chickpea Pilaf

Pears with Bay Leaves & Cherries

THIS MENU CONTAINS 626 CALORIES PER SERVING WITH 14% OF CALORIES FROM FAT.

Reduce heat to low and simmer, uncovered and stirring occasionally, until the pumpkin or squash is tender but not mushy, 20 to 25 minutes. Season with salt and pepper and garnish with yogurt.

Serves 4.

96 CALORIES PER SERVING: 3 G PROTEIN, 5 G FAT, 15 G CARBOHYDRATE; 10 MG SODIUM; 0 MG CHOLESTEROL.

Bulgur-Chickpea Pilaf

1   cup bulgur (*see* "The Well-Stocked Kitchen" *on page 221*)
1   tsp. sesame oil
½   tsp. vegetable oil, preferably canola oil
1   onion, chopped
1   clove garlic, finely chopped
1   tsp. ground cumin
1   cup canned chickpeas, drained
1   cup defatted reduced-sodium beef stock or water
    salt & freshly ground black pepper to taste

Place bulgur in a medium-sized bowl and cover with 1 cup boiling water. Let stand for 10 minutes to soften.

Meanwhile, heat sesame oil and vegetable oil in a large, deep, heavy skillet or a Dutch oven over medium heat. Add onions, garlic and cumin and sauté until the onions are softened but not browned, about 5 minutes. Stir in chickpeas. Add the reserved bulgur and stock or water and mix well. Bring to a boil, reduce heat to low, cover and simmer over low heat until the liquid is absorbed, about 10 minutes.

If the bulgur seems too wet, uncover the pan and cook over medium heat until the liquid is absorbed. Fluff with a fork and season with salt and pepper.

Serves 4.

267 CALORIES PER SERVING: 8 G PROTEIN, 4 G FAT, 51 G CARBOHYDRATE; 396 MG SODIUM; 0 MG CHOLESTEROL.

Pears with Bay Leaves & Cherries

4   pears, such as Bosc or Anjou
2   cups dry white wine
⅓   cup dried sour cherries or dried cranberries
¼   cup sugar
8   small whole bay leaves

Peel pears and cut in half lengthwise. Remove cores with a melon baller or spoon and cut each half lengthwise into thirds.

Place pear segments in a large saucepan and add wine, sour cherries or cranberries, sugar and bay leaves. Bring the mixture to a simmer. Cover and simmer gently over low heat until the pears are tender when pierced with a knife, 5 to 10 minutes.

With a slotted spoon, remove the fruit to a serving bowl, discarding bay leaves. Bring the remaining poaching liquid to a boil over high heat and cook until reduced to ½ cup, about 12 minutes. Spoon over the fruit.

Serves 4.

263 CALORIES PER SERVING: 1 G PROTEIN, 1 G FAT, 48 G CARBOHYDRATE; 8 MG SODIUM; 0 MG CHOLESTEROL.

Family Night Pizza Party

MENU

....

*Crudités with
Creamy Herb Dip*

*Double-Duty
Pizza*

*Banana-Cinnamon
Frozen Yogurt*

THIS MENU CONTAINS
431 CALORIES
PER SERVING WITH
23% OF CALORIES
FROM FAT.

Round 'em up and get 'em into the kitchen: this is a menu the family will have a good time making together. Start with fresh (and fast) supermarket pizza dough. Half is topped with stuff for the kids and half for the adults, although either mix can be doubled if you want to do just one. The kids' topping is familiar—low-fat mozzarella, tomato sauce and bacon—with one healthful addition slipped in, grated zucchini. For the adults, there's roasted red peppers, leeks and goat cheese. Before you get to work on the pizzas, blend the herb dip and slice some vegetables so you can nosh as you cook. Your youngest will have fun mashing bananas for the cinnamon-flavored frozen yogurt.

Crudités with Creamy Herb Dip

2   oz. reduced-fat cream cheese, softened (¼ cup)
2   Tbsp. buttermilk
2   Tbsp. chopped fresh chives or scallions
1   Tbsp. chopped fresh dill or parsley
1   tsp. prepared horseradish, or more to taste
    pinch sugar
    salt & freshly ground black pepper to taste
2   cups trimmed and sliced fresh vegetables (such as carrots, cucumbers, broccoli, celery, zucchini)

Place cream cheese in a small bowl and stir in buttermilk until smooth. Mix in chives or scallions, dill or parsley, horseradish, sugar, salt and pepper. Serve in a small bowl on a platter surrounded with vegetables.
    Serves 4.

46 CALORIES PER SERVING: 3 G PROTEIN, 3 G FAT, 4 G CARBOHYDRATE; 112 MG SODIUM; 5 MG CHOLESTEROL.

Double-Duty Pizza

LEEK & GOAT CHEESE TOPPING

1	leek, trimmed and cut in ½-inch slices
½	tsp. olive oil
1	tsp. balsamic vinegar
	salt & freshly ground black pepper to taste
¼	cup sliced bottled roasted red peppers (*see* "The Well-Stocked Kitchen" *on page 221*)
⅓	cup crumbled goat cheese (1½ oz.)
2	Tbsp. freshly grated Parmesan cheese

ZUCCHINI & CANADIAN BACON TOPPING

1	small zucchini, trimmed and grated
½	cup spaghetti sauce
1	oz. Canadian bacon, cut into thin strips
⅔	cup grated reduced-fat mozzarella cheese (1½ oz.)
1	Tbsp. freshly grated Parmesan cheese

CRUST

	cornmeal for preparing pan
1	lb. fresh pizza dough

Set oven rack on lowest oven shelf; preheat to 500 degrees F or the highest setting.

To make Leek & Goat Cheese topping: In a small bowl, cover leeks with cold water and thoroughly rub off any dirt. Drain in a strainer or colander and rinse again. Shake off excess water.

In a small nonstick skillet, heat oil over medium-low heat. Add the leeks and cook, stirring, until wilted, about 5 minutes. Add vinegar and 2 Tbsp. water. Cover the pan and cook until the leeks are soft and the moisture is evaporated, 6 to 8 minutes. Season with salt and pepper and let cool.

To make Zucchini & Canadian Bacon topping: Place zucchini in

Timetable

1. Make banana-cinnamon frozen yogurt.

2. Preheat oven to 500 degrees F.

3. Make dip; cut vegetables.

4. Make pizza toppings; roll out dough.

5. Assemble and bake pizza.

a strainer or colander and sprinkle lightly with salt. Let stand for about 1 minute and squeeze to remove moisture.

To assemble pizza: Sprinkle a baking sheet with cornmeal. On a lightly floured surface, roll dough into a rectangle about 15 by 10 inches. Transfer the dough to the pan, pressing to fit.

Over one half of the dough, distribute the leeks and peppers. Dot with goat cheese and sprinkle with 2 Tbsp. Parmesan.

Spread the other half of the dough with spaghetti sauce. Top with Canadian bacon and the reserved zucchini. Sprinkle with mozzarella and 1 Tbsp. Parmesan.

Bake the pizza for 10 to 15 minutes, or until the bottom is browned.

Serves 4.

248 CALORIES PER SERVING: 13 G PROTEIN, 8 G FAT, 31 G CARBOHYDRATE; 637 MG SODIUM; 20 MG CHOLESTEROL.

Banana-Cinnamon Frozen Yogurt

1   pt. nonfat vanilla frozen yogurt

2   small bananas

1   tsp. fresh lemon juice

½   tsp. ground cinnamon

Soften frozen yogurt in the microwave at medium-low power (30 percent) for 30 to 60 seconds. (*Alternatively, allow the frozen yogurt to soften for 10 to 20 minutes at room temperature.*) In a medium-sized bowl, mash together bananas, lemon juice and cinnamon thoroughly with a fork. Add the frozen yogurt and mix in well with a whisk. Scoop the mixture into dessert dishes, cover with plastic wrap and return to the freezer to firm up for about 30 minutes.

Serves 4.

137 CALORIES PER SERVING: 4 G PROTEIN, 0 G FAT, 31 G CARBOHYDRATE; 80 MG SODIUM; 0 MG CHOLESTEROL.

Great Garlicky Chicken

This homey Mediterranean chicken dish calls for no fewer than 16 cloves of garlic! That may sound like a lot, but the garlic becomes sweet and mellow after being blanched and simmered. We chose chicken thighs for their dark richness, which marries well with the robust flavors of the black olives, broccoli and garlic. The accompanying Golden Couscous with Currants & Scallions takes five minutes to prepare. For a vegetable side dish, slice plum tomatoes in half lengthwise, toss them with salt and pepper and a teaspoon or two of olive oil, and pop them in a 375-degree F oven for three-quarters of an hour. This nearly effortless method emphasizes the tomatoes' savory flavor. To finish the meal, toss ovals of red and green grapes with orange zest and juice and just enough balsamic vinegar to sharpen the flavors. If you have time, cut the grapes in half to better blend the flavors.

Chicken Sauté with Broccoli

16	large cloves garlic, unpeeled
1	bunch broccoli (1¼ lbs.), trimmed into florets
¼	cup all-purpose white flour
¼	tsp. salt, plus more to taste
¼	tsp. freshly ground black pepper, plus more to taste
1½	lbs. bone-in chicken thighs, skin and fat removed
1	Tbsp. olive oil
½	cup dry white wine
1	cup defatted reduced-sodium chicken stock
4	sprigs fresh thyme or ½ tsp. dried thyme leaves

MENU

Chicken Sauté with Broccoli

Golden Couscous with Currants & Scallions

(Roasted Tomatoes)

Compote of Red & Green Grapes

THIS MENU CONTAINS 770 CALORIES PER SERVING WITH 26% OF CALORIES FROM FAT.

Timetable

1. *Preheat oven to 375 degrees F.*

2. *Cut and roast tomatoes.*

3. *Prepare and simmer chicken.*

4. *Make grape compote.*

5. *Make couscous.*

6. *Finish chicken.*

1 tsp. arrowroot or cornstarch
8 black olives, pitted
1 Tbsp. fresh lemon juice
2 Tbsp. chopped fresh parsley

Place garlic cloves in a small saucepan and cover with water. Bring to a boil. Cook for 5 minutes. Drain, slip off skins. Set aside.

Place broccoli in a vegetable steamer over boiling water. Cover and steam until tender-crisp, 4 to 5 minutes. Remove from the steamer. Set aside. (*Alternatively, microwave broccoli with ¼ cup water, covered, on high power for 3 to 5 minutes. Drain.*)

In a shallow dish, combine flour, salt and pepper. Dredge chicken in the flour mixture, shaking off excess.

In a large skillet, heat oil over medium-high heat. Add the chicken and cook, turning, until browned on all sides, 4 to 5 minutes. Transfer the chicken to a plate and reserve.

Pour wine into the skillet and bring to a boil, stirring to scrape up any browned bits. Boil for several minutes until reduced to ¼ cup. Add chicken stock, thyme and the reserved garlic cloves; bring to a boil. Reduce heat to low and add the reserved chicken. Cover and simmer until the juices run clear when the chicken is pierced with a fork, about 20 minutes. With a slotted spoon or tongs, transfer the chicken and garlic to a platter and keep warm.

In a small bowl, dissolve arrowroot or cornstarch in 1 Tbsp. water. Stir into the liquid in the skillet and simmer, stirring, for 30 seconds to 1 minute, or until slightly thickened. Add the reserved broccoli and heat through. Add olives and lemon juice. Taste and adjust seasonings. Spoon the broccoli sauce over the chicken and garlic. Garnish with parsley.

Serves 4.

311 CALORIES PER SERVING: 27 G PROTEIN, 15 G FAT, 15 G CARBOHYDRATE; 366 MG SODIUM; 80 MG CHOLESTEROL.

Golden Couscous with Currants & Scallions

- 2 Tbsp. fresh lemon juice
- 1 Tbsp. olive oil
- ½ tsp. salt, plus more to taste
- ⅛ tsp. turmeric
- 1⅓ cups couscous (*see* "The Well-Stocked Kitchen" *on page 221*)
- ½ cup currants
- ½ cup chopped scallions (1 bunch)

In a medium-sized saucepan, bring 2 cups water, lemon juice, olive oil, salt and turmeric to a boil. Stir in couscous and currants. Remove from heat and cover pan; let sit for 5 minutes. Uncover, fluff couscous with a fork and stir in scallions. Season with additional salt if desired.

Serves 4.

320 CALORIES PER SERVING: 9 G PROTEIN, 4 G FAT, 63 G CARBOHYDRATE; 275 MG SODIUM; 0 MG CHOLESTEROL.

Compote of Red & Green Grapes

- ½ lb. seedless red grapes (1½ cups)
- ½ lb. seedless green grapes (1½ cups)
- ¼ cup fresh orange juice
- 1 Tbsp. sugar
- 1 tsp. balsamic vinegar
- ½ tsp. grated orange zest

Slice red and green grapes in half lengthwise and place in a medium-sized serving bowl. Add orange juice, sugar, vinegar and orange zest and stir to dissolve sugar. Refrigerate until serving time, about 30 minutes.

Serves 4.

100 CALORIES PER SERVING: 1 G PROTEIN, 1 G FAT, 25 G CARBOHYDRATE; 3 MG SODIUM; 0 MG CHOLESTEROL.

Unfussy Fusilli

Tender sea scallops and pasta combine with crisp fennel and a little Pernod to bring out the anise flavor of the fennel. The dish is truly a sophisticated blend of color, flavor and texture. The accompanying salad is lively with peppery watercress, slightly bitter endive and sweet red onion. A warm loaf of crusty Italian bread balances the meal. Serve strong coffee or espresso for dessert along with the Chocolate Crisps. These dark, thin cookies are flecked with bits of chopped chocolate.

Fusilli with Fennel, Scallops & Pernod

1 lb. sea scallops
1 fennel bulb
¾ lb. spinach or plain fusilli or rotini
1 Tbsp. olive oil
1 clove garlic, finely chopped
1 Tbsp. Pernod or other anise-flavored liqueur
1 Tbsp. fresh lemon juice
2 tsp. grated lemon zest
  salt & freshly ground black pepper to taste

If scallops are large, halve or quarter them, depending on size.

Trim base from fennel bulb; remove and discard stalks at the point where they branch from the bulb. Reserve the bulb and chop 2 Tbsp. of the feathery leaves. Cut off and discard any discolored parts of the bulb. Quarter the bulb lengthwise and slice thinly crosswise. Set aside.

Cook pasta in a large pot of boiling salted water until al dente, 8 to 10 minutes.

Meanwhile, in a large skillet, heat oil over medium heat. Add the

MENU

Fusilli with Fennel, Scallops & Pernod

(Italian Bread)

Endive & Watercress Salad

Chocolate Crisps

THIS MENU CONTAINS
763 CALORIES
PER SERVING WITH
19% OF CALORIES
FROM FAT.

Timetable

....

1. *Preheat oven to 300 degrees F.*

2. *Mix and bake cookies.*

3. *Heat water for pasta.*

4. *Make salad dressing.*

5. *Prepare salad ingredients.*

6. *Make sauce and cook pasta.*

7. *Toss salad.*

reserved fennel and garlic, and sauté until the fennel is crisp-tender and beginning to color, about 3 minutes. Add the reserved scallops and sauté until opaque in the center, 1 to 2 minutes more. Add Pernod and cook for 30 seconds more.

Drain the pasta and return it to the pot. Add the scallop mixture, lemon juice and lemon zest; toss to combine. Season with salt and pepper. Serve sprinkled with the reserved chopped fennel leaves.

Serves 4.

464 CALORIES PER SERVING: 30 G PROTEIN, 6 G FAT, 69 G CARBOHYDRATE; 209 MG SODIUM; 38 MG CHOLESTEROL.

Endive & Watercress Salad

....

2	Tbsp. apple cider or juice
1	Tbsp. olive oil, preferably extra-virgin
1	Tbsp. white-wine vinegar or cider vinegar
	salt & freshly ground black pepper to taste
2	heads Belgian endive, trimmed, leaves separated and broken into 1½-inch lengths
2	cups washed and dried watercress leaves
½	small red onion, thinly sliced

In a salad bowl, whisk together apple cider or juice, olive oil, vinegar, salt and pepper. Add endive, watercress and onions and toss well.

Serves 4.

48 CALORIES PER SERVING: 1 G PROTEIN, 3 G FAT, 4 G CARBOHYDRATE; 13 MG SODIUM; 0 MG CHOLESTEROL.

Chocolate Crisps

1 Tbsp. butter
¼ cup sugar
1 large egg white
2 Tbsp. all-purpose white flour
1 Tbsp. unsweetened cocoa powder
½ oz. finely chopped unsweetened chocolate (1½ Tbsp.)
1 tsp. pure vanilla extract
   pinch of salt
   confectioners' sugar (optional)

Preheat oven to 300 degrees F. Lightly oil a baking sheet or coat it with nonstick cooking spray.

In a small saucepan over medium heat, melt butter. Swirl the pan until the butter is lightly browned, about 1 minute. Transfer to a medium-sized bowl. Whisk in sugar. Add egg white, flour, cocoa, unsweetened chocolate, vanilla and salt and whisk until smooth.

Drop the batter by heaping teaspoonfuls, about 2 inches apart, onto the prepared baking sheet. Bake for 12 to 15 minutes, or until set in the center.

With a spatula, immediately transfer the cookies to a rack to cool. (If the cookies begin to stick before all are removed, return the pan briefly to the oven.)

Dust the cookies with confectioners' sugar if using.

Makes about 1 dozen cookies.

Serves 4.

111 CALORIES PER SERVING: 6 G PROTEIN, 6 G FAT, 18 G CARBOHYDRATE; 111 MG SODIUM; 9 MG CHOLESTEROL.

Very Valencian

MENU
....

Paella Rápida

Green Salad
Vinaigrette

Sherried Oranges
& Raisins

A complex, colorful blend of rice, fresh seafood and meats, paella is a traditional Spanish fiesta dish. Although some versions require all-day labor, this recipe is indeed *rápida*—without sacrificing flavor. Shrimp, tender chicken breast, artichoke hearts and roasted red peppers are tossed with the classic golden, saffron-scented rice. Smoked mussels replace the traditional pork sausages, adding depth of flavor without the fat. Bright, fun and easy to multiply, this is a good dish for company. The paella is a meal in itself; all that's needed to accompany it is a salad of greens and fresh herb vinaigrette. The fragrant, refreshing dessert is another marriage of Spanish flavors. Sherry is combined with honey, raisins and orange juice and spooned over fresh orange sections.

Paella Rápida

....

2 cups defatted reduced-sodium chicken stock

¼ tsp. saffron threads, crushed, or pinch powdered saffron

3 tsp. olive oil

½ lb. medium shrimp, peeled and deveined

½ lb. boneless, skinless chicken breast, trimmed of fat and cut into ½-inch-thick strips

   salt & freshly ground black pepper to taste

1 onion, chopped

2 cloves garlic, finely chopped

1 14½-oz. can tomatoes, with juice

⅛ tsp. red-pepper flakes

1 cup medium-grain white rice, preferably arborio

1 cup frozen artichoke hearts, thawed

THIS MENU CONTAINS 673 CALORIES PER SERVING WITH 19% OF CALORIES FROM FAT.

1 cup frozen peas, thawed

⅓ cup bottled roasted peppers, cut into strips

⅓ cup smoked mussels, not packed in oil (2 oz.)

In a small saucepan, combine chicken stock and saffron; bring to a simmer. Remove from the heat and set aside.

In a large nonstick skillet, heat 1 tsp. of the oil over high heat. Add shrimp and sauté until pink and curled, 3 to 4 minutes. Remove from the skillet and set aside.

Add another 1 tsp. of the oil to the skillet. Add chicken and sauté until lightly browned on the outside and opaque inside, 3 to 4 minutes. Remove from the skillet. Season the shrimp and chicken with salt and pepper and set aside.

Reduce heat to medium and add the remaining 1 tsp. oil to the skillet. Stir in onions and garlic; sauté until softened, 3 to 5 minutes. (Add 1 to 2 Tbsp. water if they become too dry.) Stir in tomatoes and red-pepper flakes; simmer for 3 minutes, breaking up the tomatoes with a spoon. Add rice and stir to coat well. Stir in the reserved chicken stock and bring to a simmer. Cover and cook over low heat for 20 minutes. Gently stir artichokes, peas, red peppers, mussels and the reserved shrimp and chicken into the rice mixture. Cover and cook, stirring occasionally, until the rice is tender, 5 to 10 minutes more. Season with salt and pepper and serve immediately.

Serves 4.

450 CALORIES PER SERVING: 35 G PROTEIN, 7 G FAT, 58 G CARBOHYDRATE; 423 MG SODIUM; 128 MG CHOLESTEROL.

Green Salad Vinaigrette

2 Tbsp. red-wine vinegar or fresh lemon juice

2 Tbsp. olive oil, preferably extra-virgin

2 Tbsp. defatted reduced-sodium chicken stock

½ tsp. finely chopped garlic

Timetable

1. Wash salad greens; make salad dressing.

2. Thaw artichokes and peas under warm running water or in microwave.

3. Make paella up through cooking rice.

4. Meanwhile, prepare orange segments and dessert sauce.

5. Finish paella.

6. Toss salad.

½ tsp. Dijon mustard

1 Tbsp. chopped fresh parsley, tarragon, chives or basil
salt & freshly ground black pepper to taste

8 cups washed, dried and torn mixed greens

In a large salad bowl, whisk together vinegar or lemon juice, oil, chicken stock, garlic, mustard and herbs until well blended. Season with salt and pepper. Add greens and toss.

Serves 4.

87 CALORIES PER SERVING: 3 G PROTEIN, 7 G FAT, 5 G CARBOHYDRATE; 90 MG SODIUM; 0 MG CHOLESTEROL.

Sherried Oranges & Raisins

4 large navel oranges

¼ cup raisins

2 Tbsp. honey

3 Tbsp. sweet sherry

Grate 1 tsp. zest from one of the oranges and set aside. With a sharp knife, remove the rind and white pith from the oranges and discard. Working over a medium-sized bowl, cut the orange segments from their surrounding membranes, letting them drop into the bowl. Squeeze any remaining juice from the membranes into the bowl.

Holding back the orange segments with a spoon, drain the juice from the bowl into a small saucepan. Add the reserved orange zest, raisins and honey. Bring the mixture to a simmer over medium-low heat. Cook until thickened and reduced, 3 to 5 minutes. Remove from the heat and stir in sherry. Let cool for 5 minutes.

Divide the reserved orange sections among 4 dessert bowls and spoon the sherry-raisin sauce on top.

Serves 4.

136 CALORIES PER SERVING: 2 G PROTEIN, 0 G FAT, 32 G CARBOHYDRATE; 2 MG SODIUM; 0 MG CHOLESTEROL.

From the Hills of Tuscany

D ried porcini mushrooms give this pasta an exciting, musky richness. Gathered wild from the hillsides of northern Italy, they have a warm, earthy and satisfying flavor. Served alongside the pasta are warm breadsticks. They are simple to make—store-bought pizza dough is embedded with olives and rosemary and twisted before baking. The slightly bitter radicchio salad needs just a very light and simple dressing, like this one, based on balsamic vinegar, Dijon mustard and olive oil. Plump fresh figs, pears or grapes make a lovely, unadorned conclusion to the meal.

Rigatoni with Wild Mushroom Sauce

- 1 oz. dried porcini (*see "The Well-Stocked Kitchen" on page 221*) or other dried wild mushrooms
- 2 tsp. olive oil
- 2 cloves garlic, peeled
- 1 onion, cut in half and thinly sliced
- 3 Tbsp. chopped fresh parsley
- 1½ tsp. chopped fresh oregano or ½ tsp. dried
- 6 oz. fresh mushrooms, trimmed, wiped clean and sliced
  pinch freshly grated nutmeg
- 1 14-oz. can plum tomatoes, drained, juices reserved
  salt & freshly ground black pepper to taste
- ¾ lb. rigatoni
- ¼ cup freshly grated Parmesan cheese

In a small bowl, soak dried mushrooms in 1 cup hot water for 15 to 20 minutes. Drain, reserving the soaking liquid. Strain the soaking liquid through a coffee filter or paper towel-lined strainer and set aside. Rinse

THIS MENU CONTAINS 716 CALORIES PER SERVING WITH 18% OF CALORIES FROM FAT.

and chop the mushrooms.

In a large nonstick skillet, heat oil over medium heat. Add garlic cloves and cook, stirring occasionally, until light golden, 2 to 3 minutes. Discard the garlic. Add onions, 1 Tbsp. of the parsley and oregano; cook, stirring occasionally, until the onions are softened, 4 to 5 minutes.

Increase heat to medium-high. Add fresh mushrooms, the reserved dried mushrooms and nutmeg; sauté until the mushrooms begin to soften, 3 to 4 minutes.

Stir in the reserved soaking liquid, tomatoes and about half of their juice. Bring to a boil, breaking up the tomatoes with a wooden spoon. Reduce heat to low and simmer until the juices have reduced slightly, 8 to 10 minutes. Season with salt and pepper. Stir in the remaining 2 Tbsp. parsley.

Meanwhile, cook rigatoni in a large pot of boiling salted water until al dente, about 12 to 15 minutes. Drain and transfer to a serving dish.

Spoon the mushroom sauce on top. Sprinkle with Parmesan and additional pepper.

Serves 4.

435 CALORIES PER SERVING: 17 G PROTEIN, 6 G FAT, 80 G CARBOHYDRATE; 289 MG SODIUM; 5 MG CHOLESTEROL.

Rosemary & Olive Breadsticks

Look for fresh pizza dough in the refrigerator case of large supermarkets.

- ½ lb. fresh pizza dough
- 1 Tbsp. chopped, pitted, oil-cured black olives (about 5)
- 2 tsp. chopped fresh rosemary or 1 tsp. dried
- 1 tsp. olive oil

Place oven rack in top position. Preheat oven to 450 degrees F. Lightly brush a baking sheet with oil or coat it with nonstick cooking spray.

On a lightly floured surface, roll dough into an approximate 10-by-12-inch rectangle. Sprinkle with olives and rosemary, lightly pressing them

Timetable

1. Preheat oven to 450 degrees F.

2. Soak dried mushrooms.

3. Prepare and bake breadsticks.

4. Heat water for pasta.

5. Toast nuts and prepare dressing for salad.

6. Make mushroom sauce.

7. Cook rigatoni.

8. Toss salad.

into the dough with the rolling pin. Fold the dough in half lengthwise and press with the rolling pin. Brush both sides of the dough with olive oil.

Cut the dough crosswise into twelve 1-inch strips and let rest for 5 minutes.

Pick up a strip of dough and gently stretch it, twisting it several times. Set it on the prepared baking sheet. Repeat with the remaining strips. Bake for 10 to 12 minutes, or until the breadsticks are well browned.

Makes 12 breadsticks.

Serves 4.

156 CALORIES PER SERVING: 5 G PROTEIN, 3 G FAT, 26 G CARBOHYDRATE; 277 MG SODIUM; 0 MG CHOLESTEROL.

Radicchio Salad

2 Tbsp. coarsely chopped pine nuts or walnuts
1 Tbsp. strong brewed tea, such as Earl Grey or orange pekoe
1 Tbsp. balsamic vinegar
2 tsp. olive oil, preferably extra-virgin
1 tsp. Dijon mustard
  salt & freshly ground black pepper to taste
6 cups (2 heads) washed, dried and torn radicchio (*see* "The Well-Stocked Kitchen" *on page 221*)

In a small dry skillet over low heat, stir pine nuts or walnuts until lightly toasted, 3 to 5 minutes. Transfer to a plate to cool.

In a salad bowl, whisk together tea, vinegar, olive oil, mustard, salt and pepper. Add radicchio and toss well. Sprinkle with the toasted nuts.

Serves 4.

51 CALORIES PER SERVING: 2 G PROTEIN, 5 G FAT, 2 G CARBOHYDRATE; 6 MG SODIUM; 0 MG CHOLESTEROL.

Antipasto, Pasta & Plums

T his is an Italian supper to savor with a glass of Chianti. First, there's a colorful platter of antipasti drizzled with the best olive oil you can afford. Simple and comfortable, the thick soup doubles as a bowl of pasta. Try to use fresh rosemary and good imported cheese; because only a little cheese is used, you want it to be as flavorful as possible. Crunchy breadsticks are nice on the side. Ripe plums, roasted to intensify their flavor and topped with a spoonful of their rose-purple juices, star in the dessert.

Antipasto for Six

MENU
....

Antipasto for Six

*Pasta &
Chickpea Soup*

(Breadsticks)

Roasted Plums

2 cups broccoli florets
2 tsp. balsamic vinegar
   salt to taste
1 7½-oz. jar roasted red peppers, drained and sliced
4 oz. smoked mussels, not packed in oil
6 oz. cremini mushrooms, cleaned and quartered (*see* "The Well-Stocked Kitchen" *on page 221*)
2 oz. thinly sliced provolone cheese
1 Tbsp. olive oil, preferably extra-virgin
   freshly ground black pepper to taste

Bring a medium-sized saucepan of water to a boil. Add broccoli florets and cook for 30 seconds. Drain immediately and refresh under cold running water. Toss with balsamic vinegar and season with salt. Arrange broccoli on a large serving platter with red peppers, mussels, mushrooms and provolone. Drizzle with olive oil and season generously with black pepper.
   Serves 6.

111 CALORIES PER SERVING: 9 G PROTEIN, 6 G FAT, 7 G CARBOHYDRATE; 522 MG SODIUM; 17 MG CHOLESTEROL.

THIS MENU CONTAINS
722 CALORIES
PER SERVING WITH
20% OF CALORIES
FROM FAT.

Timetable

....

1. *Preheat oven to 400 degrees F.*

2. *Prepare antipasto.*

3. *Roast plums.*

4. *Make soup.*

Pasta & Chickpea Soup

....

2   tsp. olive oil

2   cloves garlic, finely chopped

1   14-oz. can plum tomatoes, drained

1   large sprig fresh rosemary or 1½ tsp. crushed dried rosemary leaves

2   14½-oz. cans defatted reduced-sodium beef stock

2   19-oz. cans chickpeas, drained and rinsed

6   oz. elbow macaroni

½   tsp. freshly ground black pepper, or to taste

⅓   cup grated pecorino romano (*see* "The Well-Stocked Kitchen" *on page 221*) or Parmesan cheese

Heat oil in a large pot over low heat. Add garlic and cook, stirring, until golden, about 1 minute. Add tomatoes and rosemary; simmer for 5 minutes, crushing the tomatoes with a wooden spoon. Pour in beef stock and 2 cups water; bring to a simmer over medium heat.

Meanwhile, in a small bowl, mash 1 cup of the chickpeas with a fork or potato masher. Stir the mashed chickpeas into the tomato-stock mixture, along with macaroni and pepper. Simmer, uncovered, until the pasta is tender, 5 to 12 minutes. Stir in the remaining whole chickpeas and heat through. If using fresh rosemary, discard the sprig. Serve the soup with a sprinkling of grated cheese.

Makes about 9 cups.

Serves 6.

340 CALORIES PER SERVING: 16 G PROTEIN, 7 G FAT, 54 G CARBOHYDRATE; 790 MG SODIUM; 4 MG CHOLESTEROL.

Roasted Plums

8-10 ripe plums, cut in half and pitted (2 lbs.)

½ cup sugar

3 Tbsp. lemon juice

1 tsp. grated lemon zest

1 Tbsp. Slivovitz (plum brandy), or other brandy (optional)

Preheat oven to 400 degrees F. Place plums skin-side down in a 9-by-13-inch baking dish. Sprinkle the plums with sugar and lemon juice. Bake for 30 to 40 minutes, shaking the pan occasionally to distribute the juices, or until the juices are thickened and the plums are tender. (If the juices start to burn before the plums are tender, add a little water and cover the dish with aluminum foil.) Stir lemon zest and brandy, if using, into the pan juices.

Serve warm plums in individual bowls with pan juices spooned over.
Serves 6.

151 CALORIES PER SERVING: 1 G PROTEIN, 1 G FAT, 36 G CARBOHYDRATE; 0 MG SODIUM; 0 MG CHOLESTEROL.

Antipasto Options

Here are some other suggestions for the antipasto platter. Use the higher-fat choices, toward the end of the list, more sparingly.

Ribs of Celery,
thickly sliced

Carrot Sticks

Radishes

Snow Peas

Cauliflower Florets,
briefly blanched

Fennel, sliced

Pickled Cocktail Onions

Pepperoncini
(Italian Pickled Peppers)

Giardiniera
(Italian Mixed Pickled
Vegetables)

Canned Artichoke Hearts,
squeezed dry

Canned Chickpeas

Imported Black Olives,
such as Kalamata

Anchovies, blotted dry

Sardines, blotted dry

Italian Canned Tuna,
blotted dry

Prosciutto di Parma,
thinly sliced

Hard-Cooked Eggs, sliced

Winter Menus

Chicken and a Salsa Beat - 170

Spice-Crusted Chicken Breast • Lime-Orange Salsa • Roasted Green Beans & Red Peppers (Steamed Rice) • Bananas in Rum-Brown Sugar Sauce

Pork in a Port Sauce - 174

Pork Medallions with Port-&-Dried-Cranberry Sauce • Rice-&-Noodle Pilaf
Romaine, Red Onion & Orange Salad • Ginger Frozen Yogurt

Pasta & Tomato Sauce II - 177

Pasta Ruffles with Tomato-Basil Sauce • Balsamic Roasted Onions (Whole-Wheat Country Bread) • Swirled Raspberry Cream

Trattoria Taste, Pronto - 181

Linguine with Clam Sauce • Sicilian-Style Broccoli • Ricotta Cassata

South by Southwest - 184

Southwest Chicken & Hominy Stew • Quesadillas • Sangria Sundaes

A Quick Bite of Bistro Fare - 187

Beef Tournedos with Gin & Juniper Sauce • Potato Galettes • Zucchini & Mushroom Sauté
Spiced Coffee with Cognac

A Real Snappy Supper - 191

Red Snapper with Roasted Red Potatoes • Broccoli with Caramelized Shallots (Sourdough or Whole-Grain Bread) • Cappuccino Bavarian Cream

Chicken and a Salsa Beat

MENU

....

*Spice-Crusted
Chicken Breast*

Lime-Orange Salsa

*Roasted
Green Beans
& Red Peppers*

(Steamed Rice)

*Bananas in
Rum-Brown Sugar
Sauce*

THIS MENU CONTAINS
589 CALORIES
PER SERVING WITH
15% OF CALORIES
FROM FAT.

When the winter woes take hold, this dinner offers an escape: bright citrusy salsa, summery green beans and red peppers, and a rum-banana dessert. The chicken breasts are rolled in a toasted cumin, coriander and pepper mixture, broiled, then dressed with the salsa. Roasting the beans lends them a sweetly nutty flavor, accented by the mildness of the roasted peppers. The tropical theme continues with the bananas, which are simmered in a sweet rum sauce and topped with a dollop of vanilla yogurt.

Spice-Crusted Chicken Breast

....

1   Tbsp. ground coriander
1   Tbsp. ground cumin
½   Tbsp. freshly ground black pepper
1   tsp. salt
1   lb. boneless, skinless chicken breasts, fat trimmed
    (4 breast halves)
2   tsp. vegetable oil, preferably canola oil

In a small dry skillet over medium heat, toast coriander, cumin and pepper, stirring, for 45 seconds, or until aromatic. Transfer to a small bowl, add salt and set aside.

Preheat broiler. Lightly oil a broiler rack or coat it with nonstick cooking spray. Place chicken breasts between two pieces of plastic wrap; flatten the meat slightly with a rolling pin. Discard the plastic wrap. Brush both sides of the chicken with oil, then coat with the spice mixture and place on the prepared rack. Broil until the chicken is no longer pink in the center, 4 to 5 minutes per side.

Serves 4.

152 CALORIES PER SERVING: 27 G PROTEIN, 4 G FAT, 1 G CARBOHYDRATE; 611 MG SODIUM; 66 MG CHOLESTEROL.

Timetable

....

1. *Preheat oven to 450 degrees F.*

2. *Make salsa.*

3. *Cook dessert sauce until thickened.*

4. *Roast green beans and peppers.*

5. *Preheat broiler.*

6. *Cook rice.*

7. *Make chicken.*

8. *Cook bananas in sauce just before serving.*

Lime-Orange Salsa

4	navel oranges
1	small red onion, finely chopped
¼	cup lime juice
¼	cup chopped fresh parsley or cilantro
1-2	jalapeño peppers, seeded and finely chopped
1	clove garlic, finely chopped
	salt & freshly ground black pepper to taste

With a sharp knife, remove skin and white pith from oranges and discard. Working over a medium-sized bowl to catch the juice, cut the orange segments from their surrounding membrane, letting the segments fall into the bowl.

Add onions, lime juice, parsley or cilantro, jalapeños and garlic. Stir to combine. Season with salt and pepper.

Makes 2 cups.

Serves 4.

96 CALORIES PER SERVING: 2 G PROTEIN, 0 G FAT, 24 G CARBOHYDRATE; 4 MG SODIUM; 0 MG CHOLESTEROL.

Roasted Green Beans & Red Peppers

¾	lb. green beans, trimmed
1	large red bell pepper, cored, seeded and cut into long, thin strips
2	tsp. olive oil
	salt & freshly ground black pepper to taste

Preheat oven to 450 degrees F. Place green beans and peppers on a baking sheet with sides and toss with oil and salt and pepper. Spread the vegetables in an even layer. Roast for about 12 minutes, stirring midway, or until the vegetables are wrinkled, brown and tender.

Serves 4.

51 CALORIES PER SERVING: 2 G PROTEIN, 2 G FAT, 7 G CARBOHYDRATE; 5 MG SODIUM; 0 MG CHOLESTEROL.

Bananas in Rum-Brown Sugar Sauce

¼	cup packed light brown sugar
2	tsp. butter
1	tsp. vegetable oil, preferably canola oil
¼	cup dark rum
2	tsp. lime juice
¼	tsp. ground cinnamon
3	ripe but firm bananas
½	cup low-fat vanilla yogurt

In a large skillet, stir brown sugar, butter and oil over medium heat until bubbling, about 1 minute. Add rum, lime juice and cinnamon; cook until slightly thickened, about 2 minutes.

Peel bananas and cut in half lengthwise and again crosswise and add to the skillet; cook, stirring, until tender, about 1 minute.

Spoon into 4 individual dessert dishes and serve topped with a dollop of vanilla yogurt.

Serves 4.

208 CALORIES PER SERVING: 2 G PROTEIN, 4 G FAT, 36 G CARBOHYDRATE; 44 MG SODIUM; 7 MG CHOLESTEROL.

Pork in a Port Sauce

MENU
....

Pork Medallions with Port-&-Dried-Cranberry Sauce

Rice-&-Noodle Pilaf

Romaine, Red Onion & Orange Salad

Ginger Frozen Yogurt

THIS MENU CONTAINS
751 CALORIES
PER SERVING WITH
23% OF CALORIES
FROM FAT.

Pork tenderloin is always a wise choice if you seek a meat that requires minimum preparation to produce superb results. The most tender and succulent of pork cuts, tenderloin is also the leanest—almost as lean as a skinless chicken breast. Sweet port wine, balsamic vinegar and dried cranberries, stirred up in the skillet, make an almost-instant, yet sophisticated sauce that is perfect with pork. A rice-and-noodle pilaf absorbs the delicious sauce. After the satisfying pork entrée, a tossed salad of romaine, red onion and orange slices with a seasonal citrus dressing is a refreshing touch. A simple dessert of ginger-tinged frozen yogurt is a welcome conclusion to this luxurious meal.

Pork Medallions with Port-&-Dried-Cranberry Sauce
....

½ cup dried cranberries or cherries

1 tsp. vegetable oil, preferably canola oil

1 lb. pork tenderloin, trimmed of fat and membrane and cut into 12 medallions

  salt & freshly ground black pepper to taste

1 shallot, finely chopped

½ cup tawny port

¼ cup balsamic vinegar

1 cup defatted reduced-sodium chicken stock

½ tsp. dried thyme leaves

1 tsp. cornstarch

In a small saucepan, combine dried cranberries or cherries and 1 cup water. Bring to a simmer and cook for 3 minutes. Drain, reserving both fruit and cooking liquid. Set aside.

In a large nonstick skillet, heat oil over medium heat. Season pork with salt and pepper and add to the skillet; cook until browned on the outside and no longer pink inside, about 3 minutes per side. Transfer to a platter, cover loosely and keep warm. (Do not wash the skillet.)

Add shallots to the skillet and cook, stirring, for 30 seconds. Pour in port and vinegar and bring to a boil, stirring to scrape up any brown bits. Boil until reduced by half, 3 to 5 minutes. Add chicken stock, thyme and the reserved cranberry cooking liquid; boil until reduced again by half, 5 to 7 minutes. In a small bowl, dissolve cornstarch in 1 Tbsp. water. Whisk into the sauce and cook, stirring, until slightly thickened and glossy. Stir in the reserved cranberries and season with salt and pepper. Spoon the sauce over the medallions and serve.

Serves 4.

269 CALORIES PER SERVING: 26 G PROTEIN, 6 G FAT, 21 G CARBOHYDRATE; 159 MG SODIUM; 79 MG CHOLESTEROL.

Rice-&-Noodle Pilaf

2 tsp. vegetable oil, preferably canola oil
¾ cup broken fine egg noodles
¾ cup long-grain white rice
2 cups defatted reduced-sodium chicken stock
2 Tbsp. chopped fresh parsley
  salt & freshly ground black pepper to taste

Heat oil in a heavy saucepan over medium heat. Add noodles and cook, stirring constantly, until the noodles are golden brown, 3 to 5 minutes. Add rice and cook, stirring, for 1 minute. Pour in stock and bring to a boil. Reduce heat to low and simmer, covered, until the liquid is absorbed and the rice and noodles are tender, about 20 minutes. Remove from heat, stir in parsley and season with salt and pepper.

Serves 4.

171 CALORIES PER SERVING: 4 G PROTEIN, 3 G FAT, 31 G CARBOHYDRATE; 197 MG SODIUM; 3 MG CHOLESTEROL.

Timetable

1. Make dessert.

2. Simmer cranberries or cherries for pork sauce.

3. Soak onions.

4. Make salad dressing.

5. Wash greens; cut onions, oranges.

6. Make pilaf.

7. Cook pork and sauce.

8. Toss salad.

Romaine, Red Onion & Orange Salad

1   small red onion, thinly sliced
2   navel oranges
⅓   cup orange juice
2   Tbsp. olive oil, preferably extra-virgin
2   tsp. Dijon mustard
1   small clove garlic, minced
    pinch sugar
    salt & freshly ground black pepper to taste
4   cups washed, dried and torn romaine lettuce or escarole

Soak onions in cold water for 10 minutes; drain. With a sharp knife, peel oranges, removing white pith. Slice.

In a salad bowl, whisk together orange juice, oil, mustard, garlic, sugar, salt and pepper. Add lettuce, onions and orange slices; toss well.

Serves 4.

120 CALORIES PER SERVING: 2 G PROTEIN, 7 G FAT, 13 G CARBOHYDRATE; 39 MG SODIUM; 0 MG CHOLESTEROL.

Ginger Frozen Yogurt

3   cups nonfat vanilla frozen yogurt
2   Tbsp. minced crystallized ginger or preserved stem ginger
½   tsp. ground ginger

Soften frozen yogurt in the microwave at medium-low power (30 percent) for 30 to 60 seconds. (*Alternatively, allow the frozen yogurt to soften for 10 to 20 minutes at room temperature.*) Transfer to a bowl and, with a wooden spoon or whisk, stir in minced ginger and ground ginger. Scoop the mixture into dessert dishes, cover with plastic wrap and return to the freezer to firm up for about 30 minutes.

Serves 4.

191 CALORIES PER SERVING: 3 G PROTEIN, 3 G FAT, 36 G CARBOHYDRATE; 89 MG SODIUM; 4 MG CHOLESTEROL.

Pasta & Tomato Sauce II

This lovely red, white and green pasta dish looks complicated but is simple and fast. The key is no-boil lasagne noodles; no precooking needed, and they're thinner and more like fresh pasta than the usual thick lasagne noodles. The recipe for the vegetable accompaniment takes ordinary onions and transforms them into something extraordinary by adding balsamic vinegar and a bit of olive oil, then roasting them at high heat. As the onions roast (giving off a wonderful aroma), their natural sugars caramelize and blend with the vinegar. The dish works equally well with yellow onions, but the red ones are prettier. Dessert is smooth and quick, made with frozen raspberries blended with cream cheese and Grand Marnier and swirled together. Serve in a small goblet.

Pasta Ruffles with Tomato-Basil Sauce

5	oz. "precooked" 3½-by-7-inch lasagne noodles
10	oz. frozen chopped spinach, thawed and squeezed dry
½	cup plus 1 Tbsp. freshly grated Parmesan cheese
½	cup part-skim ricotta cheese
2	oz. lean ham, finely chopped
¼	tsp. freshly grated nutmeg
	salt & freshly ground black pepper to taste
1½	cups spaghetti sauce
2	Tbsp. chopped fresh basil or 2 tsp. dried

Preheat oven to 450 degrees F. Soak pasta in hot water for 10 minutes, stirring occasionally to prevent sticking.

In a medium-sized bowl, stir together spinach, ½ cup Parmesan, ricotta, ham and nutmeg. Season with salt and pepper.

MENU

Pasta Ruffles with Tomato-Basil Sauce

Balsamic Roasted Onions

(Whole-Wheat Country Bread)

Swirled Raspberry Cream

THIS MENU CONTAINS 714 CALORIES PER SERVING WITH 25% OF CALORIES FROM FAT.

Drain the noodles and blot dry. Spread each noodle with about 2 generous Tbsp. of the spinach mixture. Beginning with the short side, roll up each noodle around the filling. Cut each roll crosswise into thirds. Stand each piece on end and score an X about halfway through the roll.

In a medium-sized bowl, stir together spaghetti sauce and basil. Spread ½ cup of the sauce in the bottom of a 10-inch shallow baking dish or pie plate. Arrange the pasta rolls, scored ends up, on the sauce. Dab the remaining sauce over the pasta rolls, pressing lightly so that they open to form a ruffled top. Loosely cover the pan with a piece of aluminum foil.

Bake for 10 to 15 minutes, or until heated through. Sprinkle with the remaining 1 Tbsp. Parmesan and serve.

Serves 4.

316 CALORIES PER SERVING: 22 G PROTEIN, 9 G FAT, 37 G CARBOHYDRATE; 576 MG SODIUM; 62 MG CHOLESTEROL.

Balsamic Roasted Onions

    4   large onions, preferably red (2 lbs.)
    1   Tbsp. olive oil
    ⅓   cup balsamic vinegar
    ½   tsp. salt

Preheat oven to 450 degrees F. Slice tops off onions and peel, leaving root ends. Cut each onion into 8 wedges, taking care to slice through the root so that the wedges will stay intact.

Place the onions in a single layer in a 9-by-13-inch baking dish and toss with oil. Spread them out in a single layer. Pour vinegar over the onions and sprinkle with salt. Cover the dish with foil and bake for 45 minutes, or until almost tender. Uncover and bake for 5 to 10 minutes more, or until the onions are soft and caramelized on the bottom.

Serves 4.

136 CALORIES PER SERVING: 3 G PROTEIN, 4 G FAT, 24 G CARBOHYDRATE; 277 MG SODIUM; 0 MG CHOLESTEROL.

Timetable

1. *Preheat oven to 450 degrees F.*

2. *Thaw spinach in warm water or microwave.*

3. *Prepare and roast onions.*

4. *Soak lasagne noodles; prepare remaining ingredients for pasta ruffles.*

5. *Assemble and bake pasta ruffles.*

6. *Make raspberry cream.*

Swirled Raspberry Cream

1¾ cups frozen raspberries

1 Tbsp. sugar

2 tsp. Grand Marnier or other orange liqueur

½ cup nonfat dry milk

½ cup confectioners' sugar

4 oz. reduced-fat cream cheese

2 Tbsp. lemon juice

1 envelope unflavored gelatin

In a small bowl, stir together ¾ cup of the raspberries, sugar and Grand Marnier. Set aside to thaw for 15 minutes.

Meanwhile, puree the remaining 1 cup frozen raspberries and ½ cup water in a blender or food processor. Transfer the mixture to a fine strainer set over a bowl. Force the puree through the strainer with a rubber spatula, discarding the seeds.

Return the puree to the blender or food processor. Add dry milk, confectioners' sugar and cream cheese; blend until combined.

In a small heatproof cup or bowl, stir together lemon juice and gelatin; let soften for 1 minute. Bring a small skillet of water to a simmer. Place the cup or bowl of the gelatin mixture in the water and stir until the gelatin dissolves. Add the gelatin mixture to the blender or processor and process until blended.

Divide the raspberry cream among four 6-oz. custard cups or small bowls. Top each dish with one-fourth of the reserved raspberry-Grand Marnier mixture; gently swirl in with a teaspoon. Refrigerate until set, at least 10 minutes.

Serves 4.

192 CALORIES PER SERVING: 8 G PROTEIN, 5 G FAT, 30 G CARBOHYDRATE; 209 MG SODIUM; 12 MG CHOLESTEROL.

Trattoria Taste, Pronto

When last-minute elegance is needed, it's good to have a few cans of clams on hand. This simple sauce enlivens whole baby clams with lots of fresh basil, parsley and garlic. Toasted pine nuts add an unexpected complexity and texture to this classic Italian combination. The broccoli is simmered in an aromatic infusion of capers and garlic, which enhance its robust flavor. A traditional Sicilian dessert, Ricotta Cassata is a mellow, yet not overly sweet blend of flavors: espresso, orange, amaretto and cheese, punctuated with chopped semisweet chocolate. Although it's wonderfully sophisticated-looking, it's actually simple to prepare—a good quick dessert for company.

MENU

Linguine with
Clam Sauce

Sicilian-Style
Broccoli

Ricotta Cassata

Linguine with Clam Sauce

1   Tbsp. pine nuts
1   Tbsp. olive oil
1   onion, chopped
3   plum tomatoes, cored, seeded and chopped
2   cloves garlic, finely chopped
½   cup dry white wine
1   10-oz. can whole baby clams, drained, juice reserved
⅓   cup chopped fresh parsley
2   Tbsp. chopped fresh basil
    salt & freshly ground black pepper to taste
¾   lb. linguine

In a small dry skillet over medium heat, stir pine nuts until lightly toasted, 2 to 3 minutes. Transfer to a plate to cool.

Heat oil in a large nonstick skillet over medium heat. Add onions

THIS MENU CONTAINS
793 CALORIES
PER SERVING WITH
19% OF CALORIES
FROM FAT.

Timetable

1. *Make cassata.*

2. *Heat water for pasta.*

3. *Cut broccoli into florets.*

4. *Toast pine nuts for pasta.*

5. *Make clam sauce.*

6. *Cook pasta; make broccoli.*

and cook, stirring, until softened, about 5 minutes. Add tomatoes and garlic; cook, stirring, for about 3 minutes. Stir in wine and clam juice; bring to a simmer. Reduce the heat to low and cook for 5 minutes more. Stir in clams, parsley and basil and heat through. Season with salt and pepper.

Meanwhile, in a large pot of boiling salted water, cook pasta until al dente, about 8 minutes. Drain in a colander and add to the skillet with the sauce. Toss to coat. Sprinkle with the pine nuts and serve.

Serves 4.

514 CALORIES PER SERVING: 31 G PROTEIN, 8 G FAT, 75 G CARBOHYDRATE; 94 MG SODIUM; 47 MG CHOLESTEROL.

Sicilian-Style Broccoli

1   bunch broccoli (1 ¼ lbs.)
2   tsp. olive oil
2   Tbsp. capers, rinsed
1   clove garlic, finely chopped
    salt & freshly ground black pepper to taste

Cut off and separate broccoli florets. Trim the tough ends of the stalks; peel the stalks if desired and cut crosswise into ⅜-inch-thick slices.

In a large skillet, heat oil over medium heat. Add capers and garlic and cook, stirring, until the garlic is golden, about 1 minute. Add the broccoli florets and stalks and ½ cup water; bring to a simmer. Reduce the heat to medium-low, cover and cook until the broccoli is tender, about 5 minutes. Uncover, increase the heat to high and cook, stirring, until any remaining water evaporates, about 1 minute. Season with salt and pepper.

Serves 4.

61 CALORIES PER SERVING: 4 G PROTEIN, 3 G FAT, 7 G CARBOHYDRATE; 197 MG SODIUM; 0 MG CHOLESTEROL.

Ricotta Cassata

¾   cup part-skim ricotta cheese

¼   cup confectioners' sugar, plus extra for garnish

½   oz. semisweet chocolate, finely chopped (1½ Tbsp.)

2   tsp. amaretto or other almond-flavored liqueur

1   tsp. grated orange zest

1½   Tbsp. brandy

1   tsp. instant coffee granules, preferably espresso

24   ladyfingers (3 oz.)

In a medium-sized bowl, whisk together ricotta, ¼ cup confectioners' sugar, 1 Tbsp. of the chocolate, amaretto and orange zest until well combined. Set aside.

In a small bowl, stir brandy and coffee granules together with 2 Tbsp. lukewarm water. Brush over the flat side of the ladyfingers.

Arrange 6 ladyfingers in a row on a serving plate, flat-side up. Spread with ⅓ of the reserved ricotta mixture. Repeat two more times. Set the remaining 6 ladyfingers on top, rounded-side up. Dust with confectioners' sugar and sprinkle with the remaining chocolate.

Place in the refrigerator, loosely covered with plastic wrap, for about 20 minutes. Cut crosswise into 4 portions.

Serves 4.

218 CALORIES PER SERVING: 7 G PROTEIN, 6 G FAT, 29 G CARBOHYDRATE; 173 MG SODIUM; 14 MG CHOLESTEROL.

South by Southwest

MENU

Southwest Chicken
& Hominy Stew

Quesadillas

Sangria Sundaes

THIS MENU CONTAINS
746 CALORIES
PER SERVING WITH
16% OF CALORIES
FROM FAT.

Hominy is to corn what raisins are to grapes: a more mature, flavorful and interestingly textured version of the raw product. More familiar to residents of the South and Southwest (where it goes by its Mexican name, *pozole*), hominy is available canned in most supermarkets. Although hominy is often cooked with pork, we have combined it with chicken, seasoned it with toasted oregano and topped it with a traditional array of garnishes. Corn tortillas filled with melted cheese and topped with salsa are served alongside. The dessert, vividly crimson and citrusy, is an unexpected twist on sangria: the wine and fruit are thickened into a sauce and spooned over frozen yogurt.

Southwest Chicken & Hominy Stew

2	tsp. dried oregano
1	cup chopped red onion (1 onion)
3½	cups defatted reduced-sodium chicken stock
⅛	tsp. salt
1	clove garlic, finely chopped
1	tsp. chili powder
1	15-oz. can yellow or white hominy, drained and rinsed
1	15-oz. can black beans, drained and rinsed
¾	lb. skinless, boneless chicken breasts, trimmed of fat and cut into ¾-inch pieces
1	cup shredded green cabbage
1	lime, cut into wedges

In a small dry skillet over medium-high heat, toast oregano until fragrant, about 30 to 40 seconds. Transfer to a saucer to cool.

In a small bowl, combine 1 tsp. of the toasted oregano with ¼ cup of the onions and set aside.

In a medium-sized saucepan, combine remaining onions with 3 Tbsp. of the chicken stock and salt. Cover and cook over medium heat until the onions are translucent, about 3 minutes. Add garlic and cook for 1 minute. Add the remaining 1 tsp. oregano and chili powder and cook for 1 minute. Add hominy and the remaining chicken stock, bring to a simmer and cook for 5 minutes. Add black beans and chicken, return to a simmer and cook until the chicken is no longer pink in the center, about 5 minutes.

Serve in bowls, garnished with shredded cabbage, the reserved onion-oregano mixture and a squeeze of lime juice.

Makes 6 cups.

Serves 4.

330 CALORIES PER SERVING: 29 G PROTEIN, 5 G FAT, 43 G CARBOHYDRATE; 320 MG SODIUM; 51 MG CHOLESTEROL.

Quesadillas

   6   corn tortillas
   ¾   cup grated Monterey Jack cheese (3 oz.)
   ¼   cup tomato salsa

Heat a nonstick skillet over high heat. Place a tortilla in the pan and top with ⅓ of the cheese. Place another tortilla on top. Cook until the bottom tortilla is lightly toasted, about 1½ minutes. Turn over and cook until the cheese has melted and the other tortilla is lightly colored, about 1½ minutes more.

Transfer to a plate and cover with foil to keep warm. Repeat with the remaining tortillas and cheese.

Cut the tortillas into quarters, top with a little salsa and serve.

Serves 4.

185 CALORIES PER SERVING: 9 G PROTEIN, 8 G FAT, 20 G CARBOHYDRATE; 250 MG SODIUM; 19 MG CHOLESTEROL.

Timetable

1. *Make sangria sauce.*

2. *Make stew.*

3. *Make quesadillas.*

Sangria Sundaes

½ cup dry red wine

3 Tbsp. orange marmalade

½ tsp. lime juice

2 clementines or tangerines, peeled, segmented and cut in half

3 cups nonfat vanilla frozen yogurt

In a small saucepan, bring wine to a boil over medium-high heat. Cook until reduced to 2 Tbsp., 6 to 8 minutes. Add marmalade and cook until thickened, 1 to 2 minutes.

Remove from heat and stir in lime juice and clementines or tangerines. Let cool slightly. At serving time, scoop frozen yogurt into 4 dessert dishes and spoon the reserved sauce over the top.

Serves 4.

231 CALORIES PER SERVING: 3 G PROTEIN, 0 G FAT, 49 G CARBOHYDRATE; 56 MG SODIUM; 0 MG CHOLESTEROL.

A Quick Bite of Bistro Fare

For this sophisticated menu, pan-seared beef tenderloin takes center stage; its lively sauce, flavored with gin and juniper berries, is ready in just two minutes. The inspiration for the Potato Galettes comes from *pommes Anna*, a dish created in the 1860s for Parisian heartthrob Anna Deslions. To suit modern concerns of the heart, the butter has been stripped from the classic version: here, thinly sliced potatoes are clustered in a circle, brushed with a little oil and roasted. An earthy sauté of zucchini and mushrooms complements the main course. For dessert, there's a lovely Spiced Coffee; try it with a spot of cognac.

Beef Tournedos with Gin & Juniper Sauce

¾ cup defatted reduced-sodium beef stock

3 Tbsp. gin

3 Tbsp. balsamic vinegar

1 Tbsp. juniper berries, crushed (*see* "The Well-Stocked Kitchen" *on page 221*)

4 4-oz. beef tenderloin steaks, trimmed of fat

2 tsp. vegetable oil, preferably canola oil

1 tsp. coarsely ground black pepper

salt to taste

In a measuring cup, combine beef stock, gin, vinegar and juniper berries. Set aside.

Brush or rub steaks with vegetable oil. Press pepper onto the steaks and season with salt.

Heat a large heavy skillet over high heat until nearly smoking. Place the steaks in the heated pan and sear until browned on the outside

---

MENU

....

Beef Tournedos with Gin & Juniper Sauce

Potato Galettes

Zucchini & Mushroom Sauté

Spiced Coffee with Cognac

THIS MENU CONTAINS 490 CALORIES PER SERVING WITH 28% OF CALORIES FROM FAT.

Timetable

....

1. *Preheat oven to 400 degrees F.*

2. *Prepare zucchini and mushrooms.*

3. *Assemble and bake galettes.*

4. *Make tournedos.*

5. *Sauté vegetables.*

6. *Brew coffee; add spices.*

but still pink inside, 2 to 3 minutes per side. Transfer the steaks to a plate and keep warm.

Reduce the heat to medium and add the reserved stock mixture. Cook, stirring to scrape up any brown bits, until the stock is reduced slightly, 3 to 5 minutes. Place the steaks on individual plates and spoon the sauce over.

Serves 4.

239 CALORIES PER SERVING: 25 G PROTEIN, 11 G FAT, 4 G CARBOHYDRATE; 159 MG SODIUM; 71 MG CHOLESTEROL.

Potato Galettes

....

A food processor with a thin slicing disc makes quick work of preparing the potatoes.

4 small Yukon Gold or all-purpose potatoes (1 lb.), peeled and cut into ⅛-inch-thick slices
2 tsp. olive oil
salt & freshly ground black pepper to taste

Preheat oven to 400 degrees F. Lightly oil a baking sheet or coat it with nonstick cooking spray. To assemble the galette, overlap potato slices in a ring about 4 inches in diameter. Arrange a second, slightly smaller ring on top of the first.

Form 3 additional galettes in the same manner. Brush the galettes with oil and season with salt and pepper.

Bake for 25 to 30 minutes, or until the potatoes are tender and golden. Using a wide metal spatula, invert the galettes onto individual plates.

Serves 4.

125 CALORIES PER SERVING: 2 G PROTEIN, 2 G FAT, 24 G CARBOHYDRATE; 6 MG SODIUM; 0 MG CHOLESTEROL.

Zucchini & Mushroom Sauté

2 tsp. olive oil
2 small zucchini, trimmed and cut into ¼-inch julienne
1½ cups sliced mushrooms (4 oz.)
2 tsp. chopped fresh basil or ½ tsp. dried
salt & freshly ground black pepper to taste

In a large nonstick skillet, heat oil over high heat. Add zucchini and sauté for 2 minutes. Add mushrooms and basil and sauté just until the vegetables have softened, about 1 minute more. Season with salt and pepper.
    Serves 4.

34 CALORIES PER SERVING: 1 G PROTEIN, 2 G FAT, 3 G CARBOHYDRATE; 3 MG SODIUM; 0 MG CHOLESTEROL.

Spiced Coffee with Cognac

    brewed coffee for 4
4 tsp. dark brown sugar
3 whole cloves
1 cinnamon stick, broken in half
2 3-inch strips orange zest
2 3-inch strips lemon zest
4 oz. cognac or to taste

To a pot of freshly brewed coffee for 4, add sugar, cloves, cinnamon stick, orange zest and lemon zest. Let steep for 10 minutes. Pour into cups, holding back the flavorings with a spoon. Add cognac to taste.
    Serves 4.

92 CALORIES PER SERVING: 0 G PROTEIN, 0 G FAT, 6 G CARBOHYDRATE, 10 G ALCOHOL; 6 MG SODIUM; 0 MG CHOLESTEROL.

A Real Snappy Supper

W hile the phrase "fish-and-potatoes" might lack the comforting, stolid ring of "meat-and-potatoes," the combination makes great culinary sense. New Englanders love new potatoes in fish chowder, the French mix salt cod, potatoes and garlic for *brandade*, and the Spanish bake a whole bream on a bed of potatoes in the classic *pargo al horno*. The inspiration for this menu comes from these last two. For the main course, thinly sliced red potatoes are tossed with garlic and some olive oil, then roasted in a hot oven. During the last 10 minutes of roasting, red snapper fillets are placed on top and baked along with the potatoes. The method is a fat-cutting one: potatoes and fish share the same cooking oil. For the vegetable accompaniment, broccoli is quickly cooked and tossed with caramelized shallots; a few toasted walnuts are sprinkled over the top for crunch and character. A half-dozen common ingredients and a little kitchen magic produce a splendid Cappuccino Bavarian Cream for dessert.

Red Snapper with Roasted Red Potatoes

- 2 lbs. red potatoes (5 potatoes), peeled and very thinly sliced
- 3 cloves garlic, finely chopped
- 1½ Tbsp. olive oil, plus extra for preparing pan
- ½ tsp. salt, plus more to taste
  freshly ground black pepper to taste
- 1¼ lbs. red snapper, tilefish or rockfish fillet, cut into 4 pieces
- 4 tsp. lemon juice

MENU

·····································

Red Snapper with Roasted Red Potatoes

Broccoli with Caramelized Shallots

(Sourdough or Whole-Grain Bread)

Cappuccino Bavarian Cream

THIS MENU CONTAINS 687 CALORIES PER SERVING WITH 21% OF CALORIES FROM FAT.

Timetable

....

1. *Preheat oven to 450 degrees F.*

2. *Make Bavarian cream.*

3. *Slice and roast potatoes.*

4. *Blanch broccoli and toast walnuts.*

5. *Add fish to potatoes.*

6. *Sauté shallots and add broccoli.*

1   Tbsp. chopped fresh parsley

4   lemon wedges (optional)

Preheat oven to 450 degrees F. Lightly oil a shallow roasting pan or coat it with nonstick cooking spray. Add potatoes, garlic, olive oil, ½ tsp. salt and a generous grinding of black pepper; toss and spread in an even layer. Bake until the potatoes are beginning to brown, 20 to 30 minutes, turning them once midway through baking.

Remove the pan from the oven and place fish fillets, skin-side down, on top of the potatoes; sprinkle with lemon juice, parsley, salt and pepper. Return to the oven and bake until the fish is opaque in the center, 10 to 12 minutes. Serve with lemon wedges, if desired.

Serves 4.

336 CALORIES PER SERVING: 32 G PROTEIN, 7 G FAT, 35 G CARBOHYDRATE; 366 MG SODIUM; 53 MG CHOLESTEROL.

Broccoli with Caramelized Shallots

2   Tbsp. coarsely chopped walnuts

1   bunch broccoli (1¼ lbs.), trimmed into florets

1½   tsp. olive oil

1   cup thinly sliced shallots (4-5 large shallots)
    salt & freshly ground black pepper to taste

Preheat oven to 450 degrees F. Place walnuts in a pie plate and toast in the oven for 5 minutes, or until fragrant. Transfer to a small bowl and set aside.

Cook broccoli in boiling salted water until just tender, 3 to 5 minutes. Drain the broccoli and set it aside.

In a large nonstick skillet, heat oil over medium-low heat. Add shallots and cook, stirring often, until deep golden brown, about 10 minutes. (Add 1 or 2 Tbsp. of water if the mixture gets too dry.) Season with salt and pepper.

Add the reserved broccoli to the shallots in the skillet and toss to combine. Taste and adjust seasonings. Transfer to a serving bowl and sprinkle with the toasted walnuts.

Serves 4.

113 CALORIES PER SERVING: 7 G PROTEIN, 4 G FAT, 16 G CARBOHYDRATE; 51 MG SODIUM; 0 MG CHOLESTEROL.

Cappuccino Bavarian Cream

1½ Tbsp. instant coffee granules, preferably espresso or French roast

1 Tbsp. coffee-flavored liqueur, such as Kahlúa

1 envelope unflavored gelatin

4 oz. reduced-fat cream cheese

½ cup nonfat dry milk

½ cup confectioners' sugar

4-5 ice cubes

ground cinnamon for garnish

In a small heatproof cup or bowl, stir together coffee granules, coffee liqueur and 1 Tbsp. warm water until the granules have dissolved. Sprinkle gelatin over the mixture and let soften for 1 minute.

Meanwhile, in a blender, combine cream cheese, dry milk, confectioners' sugar and ½ cup ice water; blend on low speed until smooth.

Set the bowl containing the coffee mixture in a small skillet of simmering water and stir until the gelatin dissolves. Add to the cream cheese mixture in the blender and combine briefly. Add 4 ice cubes and blend on high speed until smooth. If at this point the mixture has not begun to thicken, add an additional ice cube and blend. Divide the mixture between 4 dessert dishes or wineglasses and refrigerate for 10 to 15 minutes. Sprinkle each portion with a little cinnamon and serve.

Serves 4.

164 CALORIES PER SERVING: 8 G PROTEIN, 5 G FAT, 22 G CARBOHYDRATE; 210 MG SODIUM; 12 MG CHOLESTEROL.

Swiss Potatoes, Efficiently

MENU

....

*Rösti Potatoes with
Ham & Cheese*

*Savoy Cabbage
with Peppers*

(Rye Bread)

*Cranberry Baked
Apples*

THIS MENU CONTAINS
694 CALORIES
PER SERVING WITH
21% OF CALORIES
FROM FAT.

This is a variation on a traditional Swiss potato cake; *rösti* refers to food that is sautéed on both sides until crisp and brown. Although that usually involves a lot of butter, this version is prepared in a hot oven and uses only a bit of olive oil. It is transformed into a main course with the addition of smoked ham and Cheddar cheese. Milder and with a more crinkly texture than regular cabbage, Savoy cabbage also has a nuttier flavor, here accented with roasted red peppers, jalapeños, caraway and mustard seeds. Baked apples filled with sweetened dried cranberries are a comforting end to the meal.

Rösti Potatoes with Ham & Cheese

....

2   lbs. all-purpose potatoes, preferably Yukon Gold (about 8), peeled and quartered
¼   cup chopped scallions (4 scallions)
½   tsp. salt
¼   tsp. freshly ground black pepper
4   tsp. olive oil
⅔   cup finely chopped smoked ham (3 oz.)
½   cup grated extra-sharp Cheddar cheese (2 oz.)

Set oven rack at the lowest level; preheat to 450 degrees F. In a medium-sized saucepan, cover potatoes with cold water. Cover and bring to a boil. Drain and refresh with cold water. When cool enough to handle, grate, by hand or in a food processor. Transfer to a bowl. Add scallions, salt and pepper; toss with a fork until mixed.

Brush 3 tsp. of the oil evenly over the surface of a 10-inch pie plate or cast-iron skillet. Spread half of the potato mixture evenly over the bottom of the pan. Sprinkle with ham and cheese. Spread the remaining potato mixture over top, pressing evenly. Brush the remaining 1 tsp. oil over the surface. Bake for about 30 minutes, or until the underside is golden and the potatoes are tender.

With a thin metal spatula or a knife, carefully loosen the edges. Shake the pie plate or skillet to be sure the potatoes are sliding freely. Invert a serving platter over the pie plate or skillet. Grasp the platter and the baking dish with oven mitts and carefully turn over. Remove the pie plate or skillet. Cut into wedges with a serrated knife and serve.

Serves 4.

362 CALORIES PER SERVING: 13 G PROTEIN, 11 G FAT, 55 G CARBOHYDRATE; 634 MG SODIUM; 22 MG CHOLESTEROL.

Savoy Cabbage with Peppers

2 tsp. vegetable oil, preferably canola oil
½ tsp. caraway seeds
½ tsp. mustard seeds
4 cups thinly sliced Savoy cabbage
1 jalapeño pepper, cored, seeded and finely chopped
¼ cup defatted reduced-sodium chicken stock
¼ cup chopped bottled roasted red peppers (*see* "The Well-Stocked Kitchen" *on page 221*)
salt & freshly ground black pepper to taste

In a large nonstick skillet, heat oil over medium heat. Add caraway and mustard seeds and cook, stirring, for 1 minute. Stir in cabbage and jalapeños and cook, stirring, for 1 minute. Stir in stock and cover the pan tightly. Reduce heat to low and simmer until the cabbage is tender, 5 to 6 minutes. Stir in red peppers and season with salt and pepper.

Makes 3½ cups.

Serves 4.

51 CALORIES PER SERVING: 2 G PROTEIN, 3 G FAT, 6 G CARBOHYDRATE; 48 MG SODIUM; 0 MG CHOLESTEROL.

Timetable

1. *Preheat oven to 450 degrees F.*

2. *Assemble and bake rösti potatoes.*

3. *Bake apples.*

4. *Cook cabbage.*

Cranberry Baked Apples

4 large baking apples, such as Cortland, Rome or Golden Delicious
½ cup dried cranberries or currants
¼ cup packed light brown sugar
2 tsp. butter
¼ cup apple cider or juice

Preheat oven to 450 degrees F. Remove a thin slice from the bottom of each apple so it will stand. Remove a ¾-inch slice from the top. With a melon baller or grapefruit spoon, scoop out the center core of each apple. (Do not cut all the way through the bottom; leave a thick shell on the sides)

In a small bowl, stir together cranberries or currants and brown sugar. Spoon ¼ of the mixture into each apple cavity. Set the apples in a small baking dish. Dot the top of each apple with ½ tsp. butter. Pour cider or apple juice around the apples and cover the dish tightly with foil.

Bake for 30 minutes, or until the apples are almost tender. Uncover the pan, baste the apples with the pan juices and bake for 10 minutes more, basting once or twice, or until the apples are tender and the juices are slightly reduced. Spoon the juices into the centers of the apples.

Serves 4.

207 CALORIES PER SERVING: 1 G PROTEIN, 2 G FAT, 50 G CARBOHYDRATE; 26 MG SODIUM; 5 MG CHOLESTEROL.

Soup Supper I: Sweden

If any people have learned how to brighten a dark winter evening, it is the Scandinavians. For this Swedish soup, the green cabbage simmers until tender in its own liquid. A little syrup brings out its inherent sweetness; the mild, low-fat turkey meatballs poach quickly in the soup at the end. Along with the soup, there are triangles of skillet-toasted pumpernickel with a zesty Fontina cheese filling, and a tart, ruby red salad of pickled beets enhanced with onion, horseradish, sour cream and dill. For dessert, we suggest fresh pears and a thin crisp Swedish gingersnap.

Swedish Cabbage Soup

1   Tbsp. olive oil
1   head green cabbage, cored and cut into 1-inch cubes (12 cups)
2   Tbsp. golden cane syrup or dark corn syrup
½   lb. ground turkey
½   tsp. salt, plus more to taste
¼   tsp. freshly ground black pepper, plus more to taste
8   cups defatted reduced-sodium chicken stock
2   bay leaves

In a heavy stockpot, heat oil over medium heat. Add cabbage and sauté until cabbage starts to release some of its liquid, 2 to 3 minutes. Reduce heat to low and add syrup. Simmer until the cabbage is tender and most of the liquid has evaporated, about 15 minutes.

Meanwhile, in a small bowl, combine turkey, salt and pepper. With wet hands, shape the mixture into meatballs the size of marbles. Set

MENU

Swedish Cabbage Soup

Pumpernickel Toasts

Pickled Beet Salad

(Fresh Pears & Gingersnaps)

THIS MENU CONTAINS 755 CALORIES PER SERVING WITH 26% OF CALORIES FROM FAT.

aside in the refrigerator.

Add chicken stock and bay leaves to the cooked cabbage mixture. Bring to a boil; reduce heat to low and simmer for 10 minutes.

Drop the reserved meatballs into the soup and simmer until they are no longer pink inside, 5 to 10 minutes. Remove bay leaves. Season with salt and a generous grinding of pepper before serving.

Serves 6.

216 CALORIES PER SERVING: 12 G PROTEIN, 10 G FAT, 16 G CARBOHYDRATE; 262 MG SODIUM; 0 MG CHOLESTEROL.

Pumpernickel Toasts

¾ cup grated Swedish Fontina cheese (3 oz.)

1 Tbsp. reduced-fat mayonnaise

2 tsp. Dijon mustard

pinch cayenne pepper

12 slices pumpernickel or rye bread, crusts removed

1 tsp. olive oil

In a small bowl, stir together cheese, mayonnaise, mustard and cayenne pepper. Spread over 6 of the bread slices. Top with the remaining bread to make sandwiches.

Brush oil evenly over the bottom of a heavy, ovenproof cast-iron skillet. Heat the skillet over medium-high heat. Add the sandwiches in batches, and cook until the undersides are lightly toasted, about 1 minute. Turn and cook the other side, about 1 minute more. Slice in half diagonally. Serve warm.

Serves 6.

199 CALORIES PER SERVING: 8 G PROTEIN, 8 G FAT, 24 G CARBOHYDRATE; 462 MG SODIUM; 17 MG CHOLESTEROL.

Timetable

1. Make meatballs for soup.

2. Make soup up to adding meatballs.

3. Marinate onions for salad.

4. Add meatballs to soup.

5. Make toasts.

6. Finish beet salad.

Pickled Beet Salad

2 1-lb. jars sliced pickled beets
1 onion, thinly sliced
2 Tbsp. prepared horseradish
2 Tbsp. reduced-fat sour cream
2 Tbsp. chopped fresh dill or parsley
   salt & freshly ground black pepper to taste

Drain pickled beets, reserving ¼ cup of the juice. In a medium-sized bowl, toss onions with the reserved pickled beet juice and let stand for 10 minutes.

Meanwhile, cut the beet slices in half. Add to the onions along with horseradish, sour cream and dill or parsley. Toss to combine. Season with salt and pepper.

Serves 6.

121 CALORIES PER SERVING: 2 G PROTEIN, 1 G FAT, 28 G CARBOHYDRATE; 462 MG SODIUM; 0 MG CHOLESTEROL.

Soup Supper II: Portugal

A warm bowl of peasant soup is a wonderful way to ease the chill of a winter night; this thick Portuguese classic is one of the best. Seasoned with garlic and spicy chorizo sausage and thickened with potatoes, it's a delicious base for the mild flavor of deep green kale. Lightly flavored with Asiago or Parmesan cheese, cornsticks make a chewy, satisfying accompaniment. To finish off the meal, try these tender, sweet apples, simmered with cider. Crystallized ginger is stirred in at the last minute to give the dish a delicious spicy bite.

Portuguese Potato & Kale Soup

2 oz. chorizo sausage, cut in half lengthwise and sliced (*see* "The Well-Stocked Kitchen" *on page 221*)

½ Tbsp. olive oil

1 onion, chopped

4 cups defatted reduced-sodium chicken stock

4 all-purpose potatoes (1½ lbs. total), peeled and sliced

3 cloves garlic, peeled

½ lb. kale, trimmed, washed and thinly sliced

salt & freshly ground black pepper to taste

Heat a small nonstick skillet over medium heat. Add chorizo and cook, stirring, until browned, about 3 minutes. Drain the chorizo on paper towels and set aside.

In a heavy stockpot, heat oil over medium heat. Add onions and sauté until softened, about 5 minutes. Add chicken stock, potatoes and garlic and bring to a boil. Reduce heat to low and simmer until the potatoes are tender, 10 to 15 minutes.

With a slotted spoon, transfer the potatoes and garlic to a bowl;

THIS MENU CONTAINS
515 CALORIES
PER SERVING WITH
30% OF CALORIES
FROM FAT

Timetable

....

1. *Preheat oven to 425 degrees F.*

2. *Braise apples.*

3. *Make soup up through cooking potatoes.*

4. *Mix and bake cornsticks.*

5. *Finish soup.*

lightly mash with a fork. Return to the soup and bring to a simmer. Stir in kale, a handful at a time. Simmer until the kale is tender, about 5 minutes. Stir in the reserved chorizo and season with salt and pepper.

Serves 4.

220 CALORIES PER SERVING: 7 G PROTEIN, 7 G FAT, 35 G CARBOHYDRATE; 204 MG SODIUM; 12 MG CHOLESTEROL.

Cheese Cornsticks

....

⅓ cup skim milk

1 large egg white

1 Tbsp. olive oil

⅓ cup all-purpose white flour

⅓ cup cornmeal, preferably stone-ground

⅓ cup freshly grated Asiago or Parmesan cheese

2 tsp. baking powder

½ tsp. sugar

⅛ tsp. salt

Preheat oven to 425 degrees F. Lightly oil a cast-iron cornstick mold or muffin pan or coat it with nonstick cooking spray.

In a measuring cup, combine milk, egg white and oil; stir briskly with a fork until mixed. In a medium-sized bowl, whisk together flour, cornmeal, grated cheese, baking powder, sugar and salt. Make a well in the center and add the milk mixture. Stir just until combined.

Spoon a heaping tablespoon of the batter into each of 8 cornstick molds or divide the batter among 4 muffin cups. Bake for 10 to 12 minutes, or until set and lightly browned.

Makes 8 cornsticks or 4 muffins.

Serves 4.

156 CALORIES PER SERVING: 7 G PROTEIN, 6 G FAT, 18 G CARBOHYDRATE; 409 MG SODIUM; 7 MG CHOLESTEROL.

Cider-Braised Apples

4 large tart apples, such as Granny Smith, peeled, cored and cut into ¾-inch-thick slices

1 tsp. ground cinnamon

½ tsp. ground allspice

½ tsp. freshly grated nutmeg

2 tsp. butter

1 tsp. vegetable oil, preferably canola oil

½ cup apple cider

2-3 Tbsp. finely chopped crystallized ginger or preserved stem ginger

In a medium-sized bowl, toss apples with cinnamon, allspice and nutmeg.

In a large nonstick skillet, heat butter and oil over medium heat. Add the apple mixture; sauté for 1 minute. Pour in cider, cover and reduce heat to medium-low. Simmer until the apples are tender, 12 to 15 minutes. Stir in ginger and serve hot.

Serves 4.

139 CALORIES PER SERVING: 0 G PROTEIN, 4 G FAT, 29 G CARBOHYDRATE; 22 MG SODIUM; 5 MG CHOLESTEROL.

Fish for Compliments

MENU

· ·

*Flounder
alla romana*

*Roasted Beets
with Mustard*

(Boiled Potatoes)

*Grapefruit with
Cassis & Rosemary*

THIS MENU CONTAINS
517 CALORIES
PER SERVING WITH
17% OF CALORIES
FROM FAT.

The tart, green flavors of this classic Roman sauce are a bracing foil for the mild flounder fillets. Gently poached in a vegetable-infused broth, the fish becomes meltingly tender, lovely on a plate next to the intensely red beets. Roasting is probably the best way to cook beets; not only is it effortless, but the beets' flavor is sweet and rich when cooked this way. Boiled potatoes, tossed with a little parsley, are a simple accent to the lively flavors of the sauce and the beets. For dessert, there's the striking yet wonderful pairing of grapefruit and fresh rosemary. The dessert is beautiful too; the segments of red and white grapefruit are drizzled with deep red crème de cassis and sprinkled with silvery-green rosemary.

Flounder alla romana

PARSLEY & CAPER SAUCE

- 2 Tbsp. olive oil
- ¼ cup chopped fresh parsley
- 2 Tbsp. capers, rinsed and chopped
- 2 Tbsp. dry sherry
- 1 Tbsp. lemon juice
- 2 tsp. fine dry unseasoned breadcrumbs
- salt to taste

FLOUNDER & POACHING LIQUID

- 1 onion, peeled and cut in half
- 1 carrot, scrubbed and cut in half
- 1 celery stalk

1   bay leaf
5-6   black peppercorns
  2   tsp. salt
  4   flounder fillets (1 lb.)

To make sauce: In a small saucepan, heat oil over low heat. Add parsley, capers, sherry, lemon juice and breadcrumbs. Stir over low heat until the mixture has a sauce-like consistency. If too thick, thin with up to 1 Tbsp. warm water. Season with salt, if desired.

To cook flounder: In a large sauté pan or wide saucepan, combine 1½ qts. water, onions, carrots, celery, bay leaf, peppercorns and salt; bring to a boil. Boil for 20 minutes. With a slotted spoon, remove and discard the vegetables, bay leaf and peppercorns.

Reduce heat to low, add flounder and simmer gently for 3 minutes. Remove the pan from the heat and let stand until the flounder flesh is opaque, about 5 minutes.

With a slotted spoon, lift the fillets from the pan, draining well. Arrange on a warm serving platter and spoon the parsley-caper sauce over.

Serves 4.

206 CALORIES PER SERVING: 22 G PROTEIN, 8 G FAT, 8 G CARBOHYDRATE; 385 MG SODIUM; 55 MG CHOLESTEROL.

Roasted Beets with Mustard

  2   lbs. small beets (12-16)
  2   tsp. olive oil
  ¼   cup sliced scallions
  2   Tbsp. Dijon mustard
  1   Tbsp. lemon juice
      salt & freshly ground black pepper to taste

Preheat oven to 425 degrees F. Discard greens from beets and cut off the stems and root ends. Scrub the beets well and cut in half lengthwise.

Timetable

1. *Preheat oven to 425 degrees F.*

2. *Prepare and roast beets.*

3. *Make Parsley & Caper Sauce and boil poaching liquid.*

4. *Cook potatoes.*

5. *Cut grapefruit; crush rosemary.*

6. *Poach fish.*

7. *Finish beets.*

On a baking sheet with sides, toss the beets with oil. Arrange cut-side down and roast for 30 minutes, or until tender when pierced with a fork. Let cool for 5 minutes and peel off and discard the skin.

Cut the beets into ⅜-inch julienne strips. Place in a medium-sized bowl and toss with scallions, mustard and lemon juice. Season with salt and pepper.

Serves 4.

103 CALORIES PER SERVING: 3 G PROTEIN, 2 G FAT, 18 G CARBOHYDRATE; 211 MG SODIUM; 0 MG CHOLESTEROL.

Grapefruit with Cassis & Rosemary

2   small red grapefruit
2   small white grapefruit
1   tsp. fresh rosemary leaves
4   Tbsp. crème de cassis (black-currant liqueur)

With a sharp knife, remove the rind and white pith from grapefruits and discard. Working over a bowl, cut the grapefruit segments from their surrounding membranes, letting them drop into the bowl. Squeeze any remaining juice from the membranes into the bowl. With a slotted spoon, remove the segments from the bowl and arrange on 4 dessert plates, reserving the juice for another use.

Slightly crush rosemary leaves with the flat of the knife blade to release the fragrant oil. Scatter over the top of the grapefruit. Drizzle each serving with 1 Tbsp. crème de cassis.

Serves 4.

122 CALORIES PER SERVING: 2 G PROTEIN, 0 G FAT, 24 G CARBOHYDRATE; 0 MG SODIUM; 0 MG CHOLESTEROL.

A Fresh Way with Salmon

It sounds *nouvelle*, but actually, salmon with lentils is a centuries-old pairing. Simmered with sweet turnips, carrots and thyme, the lentils make a rich bed for the salmon fillets, which are gently cooked on top of them just at the end. If they're available, the smaller French Puy lentils give the dish a more delicate flavor. The sprightly spinach and citrus salad is a nice contrast to the earthy lentils. Dessert is a *clafouti*, a classic French country dessert. Although it can be made from any fruit baked in a custard batter, we've chosen two in-season favorites—pears and cranberries. The dessert should be eaten warm.

MENU

Salmon on a
Bed of Lentils

Spinach &
Citrus Salad

Cranberry-Pear
Clafouti

Salmon on a Bed of Lentils

- 2 tsp. olive oil
- 1 Tbsp. finely chopped shallots
- 2 tsp. finely chopped garlic
- 2½ cups defatted reduced-sodium chicken stock
- 1 cup green or brown lentils, rinsed
- 1 small onion, peeled and studded with a clove
- 1 tsp. chopped fresh thyme or ½ tsp. dried thyme leaves
- ½ tsp. salt
- ¼ tsp. freshly ground black pepper
- 2 small white turnips, peeled and finely chopped
- 2 carrots, peeled and finely chopped
- 1 lb. salmon fillet, skin removed, cut into 4 portions
- 2 Tbsp. chopped fresh parsley
- 1 lemon, quartered

In a large saucepan, heat oil over medium heat. Add shallots and garlic

THIS MENU CONTAINS
719 CALORIES
PER SERVING WITH
21% OF CALORIES
FROM FAT.

Timetable

....

1. *Preheat oven to 375 degrees F.*

2. *Cook lentils.*

3. *Bake fruit for clafouti.*

4. *Soak onions for salad.*

5. *Cut grapefruit or oranges for salad.*

6. *Wash spinach; make dressing.*

7. *Add vegetables and salmon to lentils.*

8. *Finish clafouti.*

9. *Toss salad.*

and cook, stirring, until garlic is lightly colored, about 30 seconds. Add chicken stock, lentils, onion, thyme, salt and pepper. Bring the mixture to a boil, reduce heat to low and simmer, covered, for 20 minutes.

Add turnips and carrots; simmer until tender, about 5 minutes more. Remove the onion. Add more stock if necessary; the mixture should be slightly soupy. Taste and adjust seasonings. Lay salmon fillets on top, cover the pan and cook until the salmon is opaque in the center, 5 to 8 minutes.

Serve in shallow bowls, garnished with parsley and a lemon wedge. Serves 4.

409 CALORIES PER SERVING: 40 G PROTEIN, 10 G FAT, 42 G CARBOHYDRATE; 403 MG SODIUM; 42 MG CHOLESTEROL.

Spinach & Citrus Salad

....

½   small red onion, thinly sliced
2   small grapefruit, preferably pink or red, or 3 oranges
1   Tbsp. white-wine vinegar
1   Tbsp. olive oil, preferably extra-virgin
½   Tbsp. coarse-grain mustard, preferably Pommery
½   tsp. honey
1   clove garlic, very finely chopped
    salt & freshly ground black pepper to taste
8   cups trimmed, washed, dried and torn spinach
1   tsp. poppy seeds

Place onions in a small bowl, add cold water to cover and soak for 10 minutes. Drain and set aside.

Meanwhile, with a sharp knife, remove skin and white pith from grapefruit or oranges and discard. Working over a small bowl to catch the juice, cut the grapefruit or orange segments from their surrounding membrane; reserve the segments in a small bowl. Measure 2 Tbsp. of the juice and set aside.

In a salad bowl, whisk together vinegar, olive oil, mustard, honey, garlic, salt, pepper and the reserved fruit juice. Add spinach and the reserved onions and fruit sections. Toss and garnish with the poppy seeds.

Serves 4.

92 CALORIES PER SERVING: 4 G PROTEIN, 4 G FAT, 12 G CARBOHYDRATE; 112 MG SODIUM; 0 MG CHOLESTEROL.

Cranberry-Pear Clafouti

1   pear, peeled, cored and cut into ½-inch dice
1   cup fresh or frozen cranberries
⅓   cup plus ¼ cup sugar
2   large eggs
2   Tbsp. all-purpose white flour
1½   tsp. pure vanilla extract
⅓   cup evaporated skim milk
1   tsp. confectioners' sugar

Place oven rack in upper third of oven. Preheat oven to 375 degrees F. Lightly oil a 9-inch glass pie plate or other small shallow baking dish, or coat it with nonstick cooking spray.

Combine pears, cranberries and ⅓ cup of the sugar in the baking dish. Bake for 20 minutes, or until the fruit is tender and very juicy.

Meanwhile in a medium-sized bowl, whisk eggs, flour, vanilla and the remaining ¼ cup sugar until smooth. Whisk in evaporated skim milk.

Drain the juices from the baked fruit into a small bowl, holding back the fruit with a metal spatula. Reserve the juices. Redistribute the fruit over the bottom of the dish and pour in the egg mixture. Bake for 12 to 15 minutes, or until puffed and set. Sprinkle with confectioners' sugar. Serve warm, with the reserved fruit juices spooned over the top.

Serves 4.

218 CALORIES PER SERVING: 5 G PROTEIN, 3 G FAT, 44 G CARBOHYDRATE; 56 MG SODIUM; 107 MG CHOLESTEROL.

Scrambling for Dinner

MENU

....

Scrambled Eggs
& Red Peppers
on Semolina Toasts

Arugula-Mushroom
Salad

Prunes Steeped
in Tea

THIS MENU CONTAINS
596 CALORIES
PER SERVING WITH
21% OF CALORIES
FROM FAT

Some nights, the simple homeyness of scrambled eggs feels just right. This recipe is lighter, because egg whites replace some of the whole eggs. Flecked with pretty—and convenient—bottled red peppers, the entrée is fast too. The flavors are complemented with toasted chewy bread; any good crusty country loaf is fine, but we particularly like these eggs served over semolina toast. The salad is made with arugula, a pungent, peppery green contrasted with mild fresh mushrooms and tossed in a creamy lemon-garlic dressing. And the prunes, plain and unpretentious, are steeped in fragrant tea and lemon for a sweetly comforting dessert.

Scrambled Eggs & Red Peppers on Semolina Toasts

4	large eggs
4	large egg whites
¼	cup skim milk
½	tsp. salt, plus more to taste
¼	tsp. freshly ground black pepper, plus more to taste
1½	tsp. olive oil
1	clove garlic, finely chopped
1	7½-oz. jar roasted red peppers (*see* "The Well-Stocked Kitchen" *on page 221*), drained, rinsed and chopped
¼	tsp. dried rubbed sage, crumbled
4	½-inch-thick slices crusty semolina or Italian bread
4	tsp. black olive paste (*olivada*) or 8 black olives, pitted and finely chopped

In a medium-sized bowl, whisk together whole eggs, egg whites, milk, salt and pepper; set aside.

Timetable

....

1. *Wash arugula; slice mushrooms.*

2. *Make salad dressing.*

3. *Steep prunes.*

4. *Toss salad.*

5. *Scramble eggs and toast bread.*

Heat oil in a large nonstick skillet over low heat. Add garlic and cook, stirring, until the garlic is lightly colored, 2 to 3 minutes. Pour in the reserved egg mixture and cook, stirring, until the eggs have thickened into soft, creamy curds. Remove from the heat and stir in red peppers and sage. Season with salt and pepper, if desired.

Toast bread and spread with olive paste or chopped olives. Spoon the scrambled eggs on top of the toast and serve immediately.

Serves 4.

222 CALORIES PER SERVING: 14 G PROTEIN, 8 G FAT, 23 G CARBOHYDRATE; 622 MG SODIUM; 213 MG CHOLESTEROL.

Arugula-Mushroom Salad

1 clove garlic, peeled
¼ tsp. salt
1 Tbsp. lemon juice
1 Tbsp. reduced-fat mayonnaise
1 Tbsp. olive oil, preferably extra-virgin
1 Tbsp. chopped fresh parsley
   freshly ground black pepper to taste
6 cups washed and dried arugula leaves
2 cups sliced fresh mushrooms

Coarsely chop garlic. Sprinkle with salt and use the flat of the knife blade to mash the garlic to a paste.

Transfer to a medium-sized bowl. Whisk in lemon juice, mayonnaise, oil and parsley. Season with pepper. Add arugula and mushrooms and toss to coat with the dressing.

Serves 4.

67 CALORIES PER SERVING: 2 G PROTEIN, 5 G FAT, 5 G CARBOHYDRATE; 162 MG SODIUM; 0 MG CHOLESTEROL.

Prunes Steeped in Tea

1 lb. unpitted prunes
2 Tbsp. honey
2 tsp. lemon juice
2 3-inch strips lemon zest
3 jasmine or black currant tea bags

Place prunes, honey, lemon juice and lemon zest in a medium-sized saucepan. Add 1 cup water and bring mixture to a boil. Remove the pan from the heat, add tea bags and let steep for 3 minutes.

Remove the tea bags and let the prunes stand for a few more minutes. Serves 4.

307 CALORIES PER SERVING: 3 G PROTEIN, 1 G FAT, 81 G CARBOHYDRATE; 7 MG SODIUM; 0 MG CHOLESTEROL.

Oh, the Streets of Rome

MENU

....

Vermicelli Puttanesca

(Italian Bread)

*Greens &
Gorgonzola Salad*

*Pears Baked
in Marsala*

THIS MENU CONTAINS
887 CALORIES
PER SERVING WITH
23% OF CALORIES
FROM FAT.

With the simple-yet-sophisticated sass of anchovies, capers and olives, pasta *alla puttanesca*—streetwalker-style—is an Italian classic. This is a typical dish in a Roman trattoria, but it's quick and easy to make at home; the sauce is uncooked and can be tossed together as the vermicelli cooks.

The salad marries red leaf lettuce and peppery watercress in a vinaigrette flavored with pungent Gorgonzola, one of the great Italian cheeses. And because Gorgonzola is often served with pears, they are a natural for dessert. Baked with lemon juice in Marsala, the wine and pear juices mingle to form a deep amber syrup, which is spooned on top of the pears before serving them sprinkled with toasted almonds.

Vermicelli Puttanesca

4   large vine-ripened tomatoes, cored and coarsely chopped, or one 28-oz. can plum tomatoes, drained and coarsely chopped (3½ cups)

¼   cup chopped fresh parsley, preferably flat-leaf Italian

16 large black olives (packed in brine), pitted and chopped

3   Tbsp. capers, finely chopped

4   anchovy fillets, rinsed and finely chopped

2   Tbsp. olive oil, preferably extra-virgin

3   large cloves garlic, finely chopped

½   tsp. freshly ground black pepper, or to taste

1   lb. vermicelli or spaghettini

¼   cup freshly grated pecorino romano (*see "The Well-Stocked Kitchen" on page 221*) or Parmesan cheese

In a large pasta serving bowl, combine tomatoes, parsley, olives, capers, anchovies, oil, garlic and pepper.

Meanwhile, in a large pot of boiling salted water, cook vermicelli or spaghettini until al dente, 5 to 7 minutes.

Drain the pasta and add it to the bowl with the sauce. Toss well to combine. Taste and adjust seasonings. Sprinkle with cheese and serve immediately.

Serves 4.

580 CALORIES PER SERVING: 20 G PROTEIN, 14 G FAT, 95 G CARBOHYDRATE; 437 MG SODIUM; 5 MG CHOLESTEROL.

Greens & Gorgonzola Salad

- 1 oz. Gorgonzola cheese
- 2 Tbsp. strong brewed tea, such as Earl Grey or orange pekoe
- 1 Tbsp. white-wine vinegar
- 1 Tbsp. olive oil, preferably extra-virgin
- 1 Tbsp. finely chopped shallots
- 1 tsp. Dijon mustard
  salt & freshly ground black pepper to taste
- 3 cups washed, dried and torn red leaf lettuce
- 3 cups washed and dried watercress sprigs

In a large salad bowl, mash the cheese with a whisk. Add tea, vinegar, oil, shallots, mustard, salt and pepper and whisk to combine.

Add lettuce and watercress and toss well. Garnish with a grinding of black pepper.

Serves 4.

69 CALORIES PER SERVING: 3 G PROTEIN, 6 G FAT, 3 G CARBOHYDRATE; 146 MG SODIUM; 7 MG CHOLESTEROL.

Timetable

1. *Preheat oven to 375 degrees F.*

2. *Prepare and bake pears.*

3. *Heat water for pasta.*

4. *Prepare pasta sauce.*

5. *Wash greens; make salad dressing.*

6. *Toast almonds for dessert.*

7. *Cook pasta.*

8. *Toss salad.*

Pears Baked in Marsala

4 small pears, such as Bosc or Anjou
1 Tbsp. lemon juice
½ cup Marsala or sweet sherry
½ Tbsp. butter, cut into small pieces
1½ Tbsp. light brown sugar
⅛ tsp. ground cinnamon
1 Tbsp. chopped almonds

Place oven rack in lower third of oven; preheat to 375 degrees F.

Peel pears. Cut in half lengthwise and remove the cores with a small spoon. Rub the pear halves with lemon juice and place, cut-side down, in an 8-by-11½-inch baking dish. Pour Marsala or sherry over and around the pears and scatter butter over the top.

In a small bowl, combine brown sugar and cinnamon. Sprinkle over the pears.

Bake, uncovered, for 40 to 50 minutes, basting occasionally with the pan juices, or until the pears are tender and the juices are slightly thickened. During the last five minutes of baking, toast almonds in a pie plate in the oven until golden. Let cool slightly.

To serve, place the pears onto dessert plates, spoon the juices on top and sprinkle with the toasted almonds.

Serves 4.

164 CALORIES PER SERVING: 1 G PROTEIN, 3 G FAT, 31 G CARBOHYDRATE; 18 MG SODIUM; 4 MG CHOLESTEROL.

Take Me to New Orleans

This is a very Louisiana menu, full of Southern flavors, such as shrimp, pecans, smothered corn, greens and bourbon sauce. The crunchy shrimp is dipped in a dark beer batter and rolled in breadcrumbs mixed with chopped pecans and quickly baked at a high temperature. The shrimp becomes crispy on the outside, moist and tender on the inside—and contains much less fat than the fried variety. Serve with your favorite bottled chili sauce. We've updated traditional Southern long-boiled greens by sautéing them with a little olive oil and garlic, and spiced up the colorful smothered corn, or Macque Choux, with Tabasco sauce. The heady bourbon sauce, served over a scoop of frozen yogurt, will leave you humming a favorite Bourbon Street tune.

Beer-Batter Shrimp

⅓ cup all-purpose white flour

¼ cup dark beer

1 large egg white

½ tsp. salt

¾ cup fine, dry, unseasoned breadcrumbs

¼ cup finely chopped pecans

¼ tsp. freshly ground black pepper

1 lb. medium shrimp, peeled and deveined

4 lemon wedges

Preheat oven to 450 degrees F. Lightly oil a rack large enough to hold shrimp in a single layer or coat it with nonstick cooking spray. Put the rack on a baking sheet and set aside.

In a medium-sized bowl, whisk together flour, beer, egg white and ¼

MENU

....

Beer-Batter Shrimp

Macque Choux

Wilted Greens with Garlic

Bourbon Street Sundaes

THIS MENU CONTAINS
791 CALORIES
PER SERVING WITH
19% OF CALORIES
FROM FAT.

tsp. of the salt until creamy and smooth.

In another medium-sized bowl, stir together breadcrumbs, pecans, pepper and the remaining ¼ tsp. salt.

Dip shrimp in the breadcrumb mixture, then the egg mixture, turning to coat well, and once again in the breadcrumb mixture, turning them with a spoon to coat evenly.

Set on the prepared rack; they should not touch. Bake for 12 to 15 minutes, or until golden brown on the outside and opaque in the center. Serve piping hot with lemon wedges.

Serves 4.

281 CALORIES PER SERVING: 29 G PROTEIN, 7 G FAT, 24 G CARBOHYDRATE; 673 MG SODIUM; 222 MG CHOLESTEROL.

Macque Choux

1½ tsp. vegetable oil, preferably canola oil

1 tsp. butter

1 small onion, chopped

½ cup chopped green bell pepper (½ pepper)

1 clove garlic, finely chopped

3 cups frozen corn

1 tomato, cored, seeded and chopped

¼ tsp. Tabasco sauce, or more to taste

salt to taste

Heat oil in a large skillet over medium heat. Add butter, onions, peppers and garlic; sauté until the onions are translucent, 1 to 2 minutes.

Add corn and cook for 5 minutes, stirring often. Stir in tomatoes, reduce heat to low and simmer, stirring, until the mixture is heated through, about 3 minutes. Add Tabasco sauce and season with salt.

Serves 4.

150 CALORIES PER SERVING: 5 G PROTEIN, 3 G FAT, 31 G CARBOHYDRATE; 22 MG SODIUM; 3 MG CHOLESTEROL.

Timetable

1. *Preheat oven to 450 degrees F.*

2. *Prepare greens.*

3. *Make macque choux.*

4. *Prepare and bake shrimp.*

5. *Wilt greens.*

Wilted Greens with Garlic

1   Tbsp. olive oil
1   clove garlic, finely chopped
1   lb. spinach, washed and stemmed, or 1 lb. Swiss chard,
    washed, stems sliced, leaves torn
    salt & freshly ground black pepper to taste

Heat oil in a large skillet over medium-high heat. Add garlic and stir until golden, about 30 seconds. Add greens in batches, if necessary, and
toss until just wilted, 2 to 4 minutes. Season with salt and pepper.
   Serves 4.

56 CALORIES PER SERVING: 3 G PROTEIN, 4 G FAT, 4 G CARBOHYDRATE; 90 MG SODIUM;
0 MG CHOLESTEROL.

Bourbon Street Sundaes

½   cup packed dark brown sugar
1   Tbsp. cornstarch
¼   cup skim milk
2   Tbsp. chopped pecans
1   Tbsp. bourbon
1   tsp. butter
3   cups nonfat vanilla frozen yogurt

In a medium-sized saucepan, whisk together brown sugar and cornstarch. Gradually stir in milk; bring to a simmer, stirring, over medium-
high heat. Cook, stirring, until thickened, about 1 minute.
   Remove from the heat and stir in pecans, bourbon and butter. Serve
warm over frozen yogurt.
   Serves 4.

304 CALORIES PER SERVING: 4 G PROTEIN, 3 G FAT, 63 G CARBOHYDRATE; 78 MG
SODIUM; 3 MG CHOLESTEROL.

The Well-Stocked Kitchen

A few of the ingredients used in the recipes in The Eating Well Rush Hour Cookbook *may be unfamiliar to some readers, or not available at local supermarkets, depending on the region. Ask your grocer for help, or try a nearby health-food or ethnic specialty shop.*

ARBORIO RICE. This Italian-grown grain is a must for risotto, because the high-starch kernels add creamy texture. Arborio is now found in most supermarkets, Italian markets and health-food stores.

ARUGULA. Also called rocket, this aromatic green lends a pepper-and-mustard flavor to salads. It is sold in small bunches in the supermarket produce section or farmers' markets.

BASMATI RICE. This fragrant, nutty long-grained rice has a fine texture that lends itself to Indian and Middle Eastern cuisine. It is becoming quite widely available by the box or in bulk.

BULGUR. Made by precooking, drying and crushing wheat kernels, bulgur has become a nutritious, low-fat addition to many meat dishes nowadays. But it earned its reputation as a Middle Eastern staple in pilafs, vegetable dishes and salads, such as tabouleh.

CHINESE CHILI PASTE. Ask for it at Asian markets where you will find some of the most flavorful brands. Also available as chili puree with garlic, this blend of red and cayenne peppers, rice vinegar, salt and garlic is the base for sauces widely used in Sichuan cooking. It is now found in the specialty-foods section of many supermarkets.

CHORIZO SAUSAGE. Mexican and Spanish cookery make use of this coarse pork sausage generously seasoned with garlic, chili powder and other spices.

COCONUT MILK. The unsweetened juice made by blending coconut meat and water is a key ingredient in Thai cooking. It is not low in fat, but a little goes a long way; we have had considerable success diluting it with evaporated skim milk. Look for it in Asian markets and large supermarkets.

COUSCOUS. The tiny beads of ground wheat semolina resemble rice, but technically couscous is a kind of pasta. Most of the couscous available in North America is precooked; it requires only a five-minute plumping in hot stock or water. Whole-wheat couscous is available at health-food stores.

CREMINI MUSHROOMS. These are simply the brown cultivated mushrooms, which are becoming more and more available in supermarkets. We like them because their flavor is richer, but white mushrooms can be substituted.

CURRY POWDER, MADRAS. Madras is the hotter of curry powder types. All are a blend of 20 some seeds and spices including cardamom, chilies, cinnamon, cloves, coriander, cumin, fennel seed, fenugreek, mace, nutmeg, red pepper, black pepper, poppy seeds, sesame seeds, saffron, tamarind and turmeric. If you can't find it, substitute regular curry powder.

GLUTINOUS RICE. Also called sticky rice, sushi rice or sweet rice. The grains of this rice have a high gluten content, which makes it sticky when cooked. It should be rinsed before cooking. Available in long- or short-grain varieties. Glutinous rice is sold at Asian markets and many supermarkets.

HARISSA SAUCE. Hot chili peppers, oil, salt, garlic, cumin, coriander and caraway blend in a fiery hot sauce from Tunisia. Look for it in cans, jars or tubes in Middle Eastern markets, or substitute Indonesian Sambal Oelek.

JÍCAMA. The bulbous brown root vegetable with a crunchy white interior has been making its way from Mexican markets to most supermarkets November through May in recent years. Sweet and nutty-flavored, jícama is a great addition to any crudité platter.

JUNIPER BERRIES. The hallmark flavoring of gin, juniper berries are the dried fruits of the evergreen shrub. The berries lend a spicy, pine flavor that complements robust meat dishes. They are available in the spice section of most supermarkets.

ORZO. This tiny pasta resembles barley, the Italian for which is *orzo*. Orzo cooks up in about five minutes and makes a delightful side dish.

PECORINO ROMANO. The pecorino cheeses are made from sheep's milk in Italy. The best known of these is Romano. Although Parmesan can be substituted, pecorino Romano is preferred when a sharp flavor is desirable.

PENNE. A common tubular pasta; the name means "pens," because of the pointed nib-shaped ends. Penne are well-suited to creamy sauces and marry well with chunky vegetables.

PEPPERS, BOTTLED ROASTED. These are a convenient alternative to homemade roasted peppers. The peppers are bottled with water and salt in 7½-ounce and larger jars, and can usually be found alongside other Italian antipasto items in Italian markets and supermarkets.

PORCINI MUSHROOMS. These wild mushrooms are also known as *cèpes* or *boletes*. Dried porcini are widely used in Italian cooking; they contribute a rich, woodsy flavor to dishes. Packages of dried porcini can be found in Italian markets, specialty stores and some supermarkets.

PROSCIUTTO & PROSCIUTTO DI PARMA. An Italian ham that has been salt-cured and air-dried but not smoked. Proscuitto di Parma is truly from Parma, Italy, while some others are U.S.-Italian prosciuttos. It can be found in the deli meats section of most supermarkets.

RADICCHIO. The red-leafed Italian chicory was all the rage in salads of the 1980s, but its tender texture and slightly bitter flavor brought it beyond fad status and into supermarkets everywhere. Peak season is midwinter to spring.

SOBA & SOMEN NOODLES. These Japanese noodles are popular in cold dishes and hot soups. Soba is a dark brownish-gray buckwheat noodle popular in northern Japan, and somen is a thin wheat noodle popular for summer dishes. Some supermarket specialty-foods or noodle sections carry these, or check an Asian food store.

Metric Conversion

Metric Symbols

Celsius: C   gram: g
liter: L   centimeter: cm
milliliter: mL   millimeter: mm
kilogram: kg

Some Common Can/Package Sizes

VOLUME		MASS	
4 oz.	114 mL	4 oz.	113 g
10 oz.	284 mL	5 oz.	142 g
14 oz.	398 mL	6 oz.	170 g
19 oz.	540 mL	7¾ oz.	220 g
28 oz.	796 mL	15 oz.	425 g

Oven Temperature Conversions

IMPERIAL	METRIC
250 F	120 C
275 F	140 C
300 F	150 C
325 F	160 C
350 F	180 C
375 F	190 C
400 F	200 C
425 F	220 C
450 F	230 C
500 F	260 C

Length

IMPERIAL	METRIC
¼ inch	5 mm
⅓ inch	8 mm
½ inch	1 cm
¾ inch	2 cm
1 inch	2.5 cm
2 inches	5 cm
4 inches	10 cm

Volume

IMPERIAL	METRIC
¼ tsp.	1 mL
½ tsp.	2 mL
¾ tsp.	4 mL
1 tsp.	5 mL
2 tsp	10 mL
1 Tbsp.	15 mL
2 Tbsp.	25 mL
¼ cup	50 mL
⅓ cup	75 mL
½ cup	125 mL
⅔ cup	150 mL
¾ cup	175 mL
1 cup	250 mL
4 cups	1 L
5 cups	1.25 L

Mass (Weight)

IMPERIAL	METRIC
1 oz.	25 g
2 oz.	50 g
¼ lb.	125 g
½ lb. (8 oz.)	250 g
1 lb.	500 g
2 lb.	1 kg
3 lb.	1.5 kg
5 lb.	2.2 kg
8 lb.	3.5 kg
10 lb.	4.5 kg
11 lb.	5 kg

Developed by the Canadian Home Economics Association and the American Home Economics Committee. These guidelines were developed to simplify the conversion from Imperial measures to metric. The numbers have been rounded for convenience. When cooking from a recipe, work in the same system throughout the recipe; do not use a combination of the two.

Recipe Credits

Our thanks to the fine food writers who contributed these recipes previously published in Eating Well *Magazine.*

Jeffrey Alford and Naomi Duguid: Orange & Black Olive Salad, page 30.

Melanie Barnard: Pears Baked in Marsala, page 216.

Linda Gassenheimer: Pork Tenderloin with Keys Mango Sauce, page 16.

Ken Hom: Peach Compote with Basil, page 87, adapted from *Ken Hom's East Meets West Cuisine.* Copyright 1987 by Taurom, Inc. Reprinted by permission of Simon & Schuster, Inc.

Susie Jacobs: Romaine & Fresh Herb Salad, page 53.

Katy Keck: Zucchini & Carrot Sticks with Black-Eyed Pea Dip, page 88.

Shirley King: Vegetable Tagine with Couscous, page 52.

Bharti Kirchner: Salmon in a Vibrant Sauce, page 96; Swiss Chard & Sweet Pepper Stir-Fry, page 97; Strawberries with Minted Yogurt, page 98.

Ann Lovejoy: Peppered Lamb Chops, page 26; Rhubarb Chutney, page 27; New Potatoes & Sugar Snap Peas, page 27; Bruschetta with Tomatoes, page 79.

Perla Meyers: Salmon with Cucumbers & Dill, page 22; Chicken Sauté with Broccoli, page 151; Salmon on a Bed of Lentils, page 207.

Marc & Kim Millon: Watercress Salad, page 74; Korean Shrimp Pancakes, page 109; Strawberries with Ginger & Pine Nuts, page 111.

Leslie Glover Pendleton: Roasted Fish Catalán, page 128; Herbed White Bean Puree, page 129; Glazed Plum Tarts, page 130.

Steven Raichlen: Pork Tenderloin Southern Style, page 141.

G. Franco Romagnoli: Pasta & Chickpea Soup, page 166; Flounder alla romana, page 204; Vermicelli Puttanesca, page 214.

Richard Sax: Rigatoni with Wild Mushroom Sauce, page 161.

Elizabeth Schneider: Penne with Sugar Snap Peas, page 106.

Regina Schrambling: Whole-Wheat Couscous Pilaf, page 29; Bulgur-Chickpea Pilaf, page 146; Cider-Braised Apples, page 203; Black-Eyed Pea & Artichoke Salad, page 143.

Andrew Silva: Southwest Chicken & Hominy Stew, page 184; Quesadillas, page 185; Sangria Sundaes, page 186.

Jude W. Theriot: Macque Choux, page 219.

John Willoughby and Chris Schlesinger: Tuna with Scallion-Ginger Relish, page 71; Chicken Yucatan, page 75, adapted from *Big Flavors of the Hot Sun* (William Morrow, 1994); Caribbean Rice & Beans, page 76; Broiled Pineapple, page 77, adapted from *Big Flavors of the Hot Sun;* Pumpkin & Tomato Curry, page 145, adapted from *Big Flavors of the Hot Sun;* Lime-Orange Salsa, page 172.

Accessories

Page 47: Cutlery, bowl and plate from Pottery Barn, (800) 922-5507.

Page 93: Lantern from Pottery Barn.

Page 113: Plates from Pottery Barn.

Page 162: Bowl from Ceramica, (800) 228-0858.

Page 218: Plate from Ceramica.

Recipe Index

Page numbers in italics indicate photographs

More Cookbooks from

EatingWell BOOKS

The Eating Well Recipe Rescue Cookbook

High-Fat Favorites Transformed Into Healthy Low-Fat Favorites

Edited by
Patricia Jamieson & Cheryl Dorschner

ISBN 1-884943-00-4 (hardcover) $24.95
ISBN 1-884943-01-2 (paperback) $15.95

The Eating Well Cookbook

A Deluxe Collection of EATING WELL's *Finest Recipes*

Edited by
Rux Martin, Patricia Jamieson & Elizabeth Hiser

ISBN 1-884943-02-0 (hardcover) $24.95
ISBN 1-884943-03-9 (paperback) $15.95